The Myth of Addiction
Second Edition

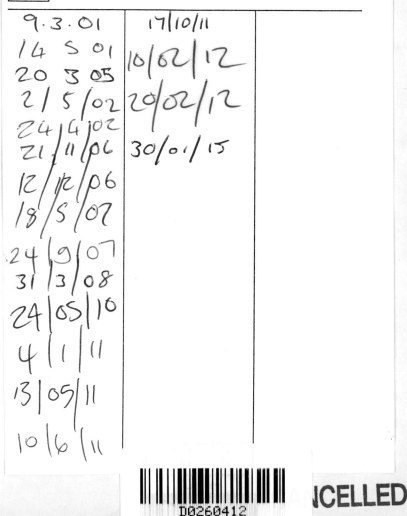

The Myth of Addiction
Second Edition

John Booth Davies
University of Strathclyde, UK

 harwood academic publishers

Australia • Canada • China • France • Germany • India
Japan • Luxembourg • Malaysia • The Netherlands • Russia
Singapore • Switzerland • Thailand • United Kingdom

Copyright © 1992, 1997 OPA (Overseas Publishers Association) Amsterdam B.V. Published in The Netherlands by Harwood Academic Publishers.

First Edition published 1992
Second Edition published 1997

Amsteldijk 166
1st Floor
1079 LH Amsterdam
The Netherlands

British Library Cataloguing in Publication Data

Davies, John Booth
  The myth of addiction. – 2nd ed.
  1. Narcotic habit
  I. Title
  362.2'93

ISBN: 90-5702-237-0

CONTENTS

I wrote this book because I wanted to. Nobody made me do it,
and I did it on purpose.
· I was certainly not forced into it by circumstances.
Finally, I wrote it for me. It would be dishonest to attribute it to
some other person.

Preface to the Second Edition

The first edition of *The Myth of Addiction* appeared in 1992, and
expressed my conviction that the view taken of the state we describe as
'addicted' is too mechanistic and too remote from the realm of human
desires and purposes, too often. Instead of a view of addiction problems as deriving from the interaction of a substance, a setting, and the
aims and goals of those who use the substance (i.e. a view that sees
addiction as something that people *do*), the prevailing notions tend to
see addiction as something that *happens to people*; that is, as something
imposed from outside by the inescapable pharmacological properties
of an alien substance, rather than as a state negotiated through the
more understandable channels of human desire and intention. Central
to this argument were certain observed facts concerning attribution
theory, and the ways in which people explain their actions. From the
standpoint of functional attribution, the reasons people give for their
drug use are not, and never can be, hard or so-called 'objective' data
on why drug use happens. Consequently, the use of such statements as
criteria against which to validate physiological or other measures, or as
factual statements from which to derive diagnostic criteria, is probably
misconceived. *The Myth of Addiction* argues that such explanations are
primarily functional. Explaining one's behaviour as either within, or
outwith, one's control has either positive or negative consequences according to the situation and in a climate of moral and legal censure it
makes sense to choose the latter.

Not everyone agrees with these propositions. However, whenever I meet someone who has read the first edition, I usually find that it has provoked a reaction; sometimes positive, sometimes negative, and sometimes somewhere in-between. And on odd occasions, people have even found it necessary to make unsolicited statements about the book in order to let others know how much they agreed, or disagreed with it. However, regardless of outcome, I thank everyone who bothered to comment for their views and for having spent time in thinking about the issues raised. If *The Myth*. . .provoked *any* reaction, I am well pleased whenever someone has been sufficiently energetic and interested to read it.

I am particularly pleased that a second edition is now considered desirable. Since the first edition, the application of attribution theory to addiction problems has developed somewhat, so there have been a few minor revisions. The intention remains the same, however; simply to put back some humanity and comprehensibility into a process too often seen as arising from the magical power of drugs to change the very bases of human behaviour, regardless of the goals and purposes of the user.

Prologue

One of the difficulties with putting across messages about drug use is that the problem is more complicated than many of us would like to believe. The drug issue usually attracts our attention through media presentations which seek to reduce the issue to a single, instantly comprehensible message but in the process an inaccurate and largely false impression is created. Even amongst many drug workers and researchers, there is an avoidance of anything that smacks of theory, and a preference for action, even if that action is based on nothing more than personal prejudice and guesswork.

Furthermore, stereotyped and inaccurate views of addiction are not uncommon even within the ranks of those who work intimately with drug problems, where there is all too frequently a lack of coherence in terms of the work carried out, and an unwillingness to consider alternative interpretations. Perhaps most of all, there is the belief that the 'truth' about the nature and causes of addiction can be revealed by methods which rely principally on asking people to answer questions or express opinions about their own or other people's drug use.

However, answering questions and stating opinions are behaviours in their own right, which have dynamics all of their own. For these reasons, it is important to consider existing knowledge on the way people answer questions and explain their actions, since understanding these processes may yield fresh perspectives on the issue under investigation. The present book attempts to provide such an alternative perspective in the area of drug use and misuse. Whilst the ideas contained are not new, they represent a species of argument which is neglected, primarily because it is slightly more complicated than the more popular theories of drug use.

The argument presented in the following pages is basically that people take drugs because they want to and because it makes sense for them to do so given the choices available, rather than because they are compelled to by the pharmacology of the drugs they take. Nonetheless, we generally prefer to conceptualise our drug abusers in terms which imply that their behaviour is not their own to control. This picture arises because it is the picture we *want to have*, and the view is supported by a body of data consisting largely of people's self reports, opinions and statements of belief. This body of data, whilst potentially of great value in certain respects, is frequently put to uses for which it is ill suited; it does not always mean what we think it means.

When asked questions by members of the research establishment, it is functional for drug users to report that they are addicted, forced into theft, harassed by stressful life events, and driven into drug use by forces beyond their capacity to control. The central argument of this book is that such self reports have their own internal functional logic which is independent of reality, and that other research methods and forms of analysis would consequently produce a different picture. Furthermore, the fact that the explanations people provide for their behaviour make some reference to their own motives and intentions is hardly new; it is a central feature of social interaction, and not specific to drug users.

At the present moment, the standard line taken by a majority of people in the media, in treatment agencies, in government and elsewhere, hinges around notions of the helpless addict who has no power over his/her behaviour; and the evil pusher lurking on street corners, trying to ensnare the nation's youth. They are joined together in a deadly game by a variety of pharmacologically active substances whose addictive powers are so great that to try them is to become addicted almost at once. Thereafter, life becomes a nightmare of withdrawal symptoms, involuntary theft, and a compulsive need for drugs which cannot be controlled. In fact, not one of these things is, or rather needs to be, true.

Whilst availability is probably a major determinant of the extent of drug use, the precise form taken by drug problems within any given society is determined in large part by that society's response to the problem. Consequently, if we were to observe that within some fairly limited time span a particular drug had become a matter of life-and-death on the streets, this would probably indicate that the policies we were currently implementing were extremely dangerous; more dangerous in fact than the drugs we were attempting to stamp out. Unfortunately, our own legislators look for advice with frightening regularity to nations where the attempt to control drug use has had the most grotesque and spectacular consequences, in the mistaken assumption that they have thereby demonstrated some sort of competence in this field.

If we continue to base our policies on stereotypes and inaccurate perceptions of the helpless junkie, the evil pusher, and the substance with the capacity to enslave, we are already half-way to justifying the most extreme measures in order to eliminate drug use from our midst. If we persist in this lethal spiral, we can bring death and street warfare into our midst, in a manner that will mirror similar developments elsewhere.

In fact, as the following chapters will attempt to show, our beliefs about drugs and drug users are largely inaccurate. We choose to believe in helpless junkies and evil pushers primarily because we want to believe in them, and because such beliefs serve functions for us. The helpless junkie only exists because we all want him/her to exist; and because drug research continues to make naive use of what people say about their addictions. It is now imperative that we start to view research based on what drug-users say about themselves in its true light; and in consequence, to expect something more dynamic and positive from those of us who encounter drug problems. The interrelationship of IV drug use with HIV/AIDS makes such a new dynamic and purposive perspective essential.

What the book says, basically, is that most people who use drugs do so for their own reasons, on purpose, because they like it, and because they find no adequate reason for not doing so; rather than because they fall prey to some addictive illness which removes their capacity for voluntary behaviour. The book then points out the reasons why the second type of explanation is nonetheless more popular and is generally preferred; and why scientists and practitioners frequently seek out evidence relevant to that view rather than to any other and subsequently impose it on their clientele for reasons that have nothing to do with scientific knowledge. It is then argued that a different context or 'system' is required within which an alternative view of drug use can thrive; a view which stresses volition and control deriving from the ability to make and implement personal decisions.

What the book does not say is that drugs have no pharmacological effect; nor does it deny that some individuals become terribly enmeshed in a cycle of substance use and misuse, sometimes with tragic consequences. The reader should note, however, that deaths due to illicit drug use per annum are generally in the order of 300-400. For comparison, smoking accounts for some 100,000 deaths; and whilst figures for alcohol-related deaths are more problematic, there are 17,500 admissions to psychiatric hospitals due to alcohol, and the direct effects of alcohol are implicated in three out of four of all deaths due to liver disease (The Royal College of Psychiatrists 1986; 1987). The drugs we regard as socially acceptable and that many of us use in a more-or-less habitual fashion can hardly be regarded as 'safe'.

The final message is that dealing with drug problems rationally depends on giving back to people the sense of personal power and volition which they require if they are to control their drug use for themselves; a power which existing concepts of 'addiction' frequently seek to limit or deny at the outset as a precondition to further treatment. To take this apparently simple step, however, involves a major rethinking of contemporary moral attitudes to drugs and addiction, since these shape the nature of the help that we are prepared to offer. In the meantime, the existing system does not work. There is little indication that anything on offer at the moment does better than spontaneous recovery (that is, giving up all by yourself); and some evidence that punitive legislative interventions make things worse by institutionalising the type of harmful drug use that we most wish to avoid.

1
Attribution Theory: Explaining Explanation

Attribution theory is a general title for a body of theory and research into the ways in which people explain why things happen. By and large the bulk of the work has confined itself to the explanations that people offer for various types of human behaviour, rather than the behaviour of objects, animals or natural forces, and this preoccupation probably reflects Western conceptions and values about the nature of the world. For religious and other reasons, we tend to view ourselves as the focus or centre of the Universe, or as the high point of creation, and hence attribution theory has concentrated on the explanation of human behaviour to the relative neglect of other things. It is clear that from other cultural perspectives, which see humans as part of a larger purposive universal process with a will and/or direction of its own, attribution theory would take a different and rather interesting turn; for example, certain central precepts would simply not make sense from such a perspective (Jahoda 1979).

Nonetheless, within our own cultural framework, attribution theory has offered important insights into the ways in which people explain their own actions and the actions of others; and in the course of that process light has coincidentally been shed on the difference between causal explanations as social constructions (reasons) and causal explanations as scientific statements (causes).

For example, the 'reason' for a particular action is frequently a verbal statement made by an individual when asked a question by a third party, such as 'Why did you do this?', or 'Why did she do

1

that?'. In answering the question the motives, affiliations, intentions and self-perceptions of the person doing the explaining are often reflected in the type of explanation offered. This is regularly seen in party political broadcasts, when members of a governing party explain unpopular policies by reference to circumstances beyond their control; perhaps making use of sentences that begin , 'We in the XXXXXXX party had no choice but to do this because. . . . . .'. On the other hand, popular policies will be explained by reference to internal qualities such as compassion, concern or goodness, and an explanation might lead with, 'We in the XXXXXXX party did this because we felt it was high time that something was done to help the situation of. . . . . .'. Such explanations are easily seen to be primarily social constructions with clear purposes and functions for the person doing the explaining; specifically, the avoidance of blame and the accumulation of personal credit.

By contrast, within our idealised conception of science (see for example the Logical Empiricist view of science advanced by Popper 1959) the question 'Why does water turn to steam when it boils?' is presumed to elicit a scientific statement of 'causality' that is independent of the motives, intentions and self-perceptions of the scientist doing the explaining (an assumption that is by no means true – see for example Kuhn 1970). From this idealised scientific viewpoint, it is assumed that different scientists will offer the same causal account regardless of their own motives, dispositions and propensities; that the explanation will represent the state of knowledge rather than the state of the explainer; and that in some sense the explanation offered will be 'real' or 'absolute'.

Unfortunately, we sometimes lose sight of the distinction between causal accounts that are socially functional, and those which are scientifically functional, and the two become intermingled. Thus we may try to shed light on the *causes* of theft amongst drug users by asking them to tell us their *reasons* for stealing; or to investigate the *causes* of relapse amongst alcohol abusers by asking them their *reasons* for relapsing. In other words, we can fall into the trap of assuming that reasons provide a shortcut to discovering causes. Even more problematic is the fact that sometimes it is difficult to know which type of account we are dealing with, and that in real-life situations the two may be closely interwoven.

However, by becoming involved in this discussion of social

versus scientific explanations we have to some extent jumped the gun. Originally, attribution theory sought to shed light on the nature of people's explanations for everyday events without distinguishing between the social nature of reasons and the scientific nature of causes. These were lumped together under a general banner of 'causal explanations', and it is to this earlier work that we must now turn in order to grasp the fundamental principles of attribution.

The Bases of Attribution Theory

Several accounts of the multi-faceted pedigree of attribution theory are available for the reader wishing to go into more detail than is provided in this chapter. Two of the best are given by Antaki (1982), and by Hewstone (1983) and it is worthwhile highlighting the salient features from these accounts.

The basis for attribution theory is the desire to understand how people arrive at common-sense explanations for their own and for others behaviour. The original stimulus for the work came from Heider (1958) in a much-cited work, *The Psychology of Interpersonal Relations*, in which it was suggested that a major task for anyone trying to understand the social and physical world was to produce satisfactory accounts of why things happened. Insofar as this applied to understanding why people do the things they do, this amounted to finding satisfactory causal accounts of behaviour; and furthermore, since searching for explanations is something that scientists do, this amounted to regarding people as if they were in some sense natural or primitive psychologists. From this basis, the idea of man as a naive scientist began to emerge, this notion deriving from the accumulating evidence that people made inferences about the causes of human behaviour on the basis of their observations of social acts, in the way that the scientist or physicist makes inferences on the basis of observations of physical events. The task then became one of finding out how such causal inferences were made, and illuminating the kinds of evidence involved in the process.

More importantly however these causal inferences, 'describing and predicting events as a science should do' (Hewstone *op cit*), were held to have important implications for behaviour *whether they were 'true' or not*. With respect to addiction, for example, this would imply that belief in the inability of addicts to control their own drug use, would have important behavioural implications whether such a belief were true or not.

Attribution as Lawful Explanation

Subsequent to Heider's original ideas, Jones and Davis (1965) are usually credited with making the next major step forward with their theory of 'correspondent inferences'. This theory sought to explain how far a person's actions could be accounted for in terms of the traits, dispositions and intentions of the person doing the act (known in attributional parlance as the 'actor'), rather than in terms of situational or other 'external' factors. The empirical work on this topic centred around 'common and non-common effects', and the reader is referred to either of the two texts cited above for an explanation of these terms.

However, the development by Kelley (1967) of the ANOVA model of causal inference merits closer inspection within this present text, because it presents a very clear picture of the type of thinking which can underlie the construction of causal explanations of human action. The model conceptualises the causal attribution process as hinging around the covariation of three dimensions, the title of this theoretical approach (the 'ANOVA' model of attribution) deriving from a loose analogy with analysis of variance. Kelley's approach is particularly useful as it illustrates one of the central features of attribution theories in a very graphic and comprehensible manner; namely, the fact that the explanation postulated for some action results from the way in which that situation is perceived by the person constructing the causal account (the 'observer').

Kelley's formulation of the attributional process was first revealed in a widely-read paper presented at the Nebraska Symposium on Motivation, in 1967. He proposed that the type of explanation a person is likely to offer for an observed piece of social behaviour depends on the interaction (the "covariation and configuration") of three factors. At risk of doing some violence to the original conceptions, the three factors Kelley proposed were in essence:

i) *consensus* – given that I have seen this person doing this thing, are other people doing it also? To the extent that the answer is "yes", there is high consensus. If "no", there is low consensus. ii) *consistency* – does this person do this thing repeatedly, or regularly? To the extent that the answer is "yes" there is high consistency. If the behaviour is rare or a single instance, there is low consistency. iii) *distinctiveness* – consider the object of this behaviour. Usually, this is the person who is having this thing done to them. Is he/ she the sole recipient, or do other people have this done to them also? To the extent that the object person is unique, there is high distinctiveness. To the extent that he/she is only one of a number who receive this treatment, there is low distinctiveness.

It is important to bear in mind that information about consensus, consistency and distinctiveness can come to the observer through channels other than direct observation. Regardless of Heider's, Jones and Davis's, or Kelley's original intentions, the general model does not in principle appear to require first hand information, but can be applied to reported information, or even to beliefs or preconceptions (referred to in the literature as "causal schemata") formed in the absence of literal multiple observations. Whilst attribution theorists sometimes conceptualise such a situation as one of *incomplete data*, this is perhaps misleading if we thereby conclude that the resulting causal account must, as a consequence, necessarily be less powerful or persuasive than one based on direct observation. In fact a persons beliefs about, say, the consistency of an act (for example, that "alcoholics" inevitably relapse after one drink) can be plugged into the model as readily as can direct observations, where their influence will be as powerful as direct observations if the beliefs in question are sufficiently strongly held.

Whilst the detailed explication of Kelley's system can become almost as complex as one wishes to make it, a process involving independent consideration of "persons, entities, and time" and their interactions, in practice it is easy to elucidate at a basic level in the following way.

Suppose we observe one day that Tom is hitting Mary, and that we have information available (of whatever type – observations, second-hand reports, stereotypes, prejudices etc.) about the pattern of consensus, consistency and distinctiveness surrounding this act. For example, it is just Tom who hits Mary (low consensus), he seems to hit Mary quite often (high consistency) and he also hits other girls (low distinctiveness). In these circumstances, we are likely to explain the event in terms of a negative property of Tom; he is aggressive, unpleasant, a bully, and so forth.

Imagine, however, that our information suggests high consensus (other children also hit Mary); high consistency (they hit her often); and these children are not generally noted for hitting other people (high distinctiveness). In these circumstances, we are likely to attribute the act to some disposition of Mary; perhaps for example there is something she repeatedly does that tests everyone's patience. Whatever the truth of the matter, we are likely to attribute the behaviour to a negative property of Mary.

Developing the above lines of argument, it is easy to conceptualise the Tom-hits-Mary scene in tabular form as follows, with each of the three variables being potentially high (HI) or low (LO), leading thereby to particular types of explanations for the observed act.

TOM HITS MARY.

consensus	HI	or	LO
consistency	HI	or	LO
distinctiveness	HI	or	LO

Using Kelley's three dimensions, we have seen how the pattern LO, HI, LO leads to explanation in terms of negative attributions about Tom; whilst HI,HI,HI leads to negative attributions about Mary. It is amusing and instructive to consider other alternatives, and to try and predict the type of explanation which might be forthcoming. Some patterns are quite easy, others are more subtle. For example, HI, LO,HI implies that there are *particular situations* in which Mary gets on everyone's nerves (i.e. a person x situation interaction); and LO, LO, HI suggests that the incident was due to some *unfortunate and unforeseeable circumstance*.

These simple examples based on Kelley's notions serve to illustrate two of the general points made earlier. Firstly, people construct explanations of social behaviour in a manner which is psychologically dynamic rather than primarily veridical. In fact, the attribution process has nothing to say on the issue of whether explanations constructed in these terms are true or not. Secondly, the process also appears to be lawful, Kelley suggesting a way of conceptualising it in terms of three major building blocks out of which explanation is formed in a logical or quasi-logical fashion.

Viewed in this way, social explanation is not based on any knowledge of actual causality, but is an inference made on the basis of certain social features of the act about which the observer has information of some kind. Consequently, the account might be "true" or not. In addition, as we shall see later, this approach is not specific to the explanation of other people's behaviour, since there is research indicating that the explanation of *our own* actions can also be handled within the attributional perspective.

The Work of Michotte and Heider on the Perception of Causality

In tracing the development of attribution theory, however, it is useful to go back to Heider and consider the influence of Gestalt psychology and specifically certain experiments by Michotte (1946) into "phenomenal causality" which clearly influenced Heider's thinking. In the cited studies, Michotte was primarily interested in perceptual processes, notably visual perception. Within that historical context, the word perception retained its classical meaning and was considered to be distinct from cognition. It certainly had none of the social-cognitive implications of more modern usages as embodied in phrases like "interpersonal perception". Nonetheless, Michotte's studies elegantly illustrate the manner in which perception and cognition are closely intertwined.

Michotte investigated the ways in which people *perceived causality*. His experiments used visual stimuli consisting of combinations of blobs, circles, squares and lines which appeared to move in certain ways; Michotte achieving his visual effects by means of revolving discs on which were drawn distorted circles, only portions of which could be observed through a slot. In one example, a small black square would proceed across a plain visual field towards a second, stationary, square. The first square would appear to strike the second. After the apparent impact, the second square would move away in the same direction whilst the first one would stop. When viewing this and other similar visual arrays, people would describe the events in causal terms. The movement of the second square would be seen as *caused* by the impact of the first square. In a similar way, other stimuli would give rise to the phenomenological impression of a causal chain of events when visual representations of objects (usually geometrical shapes) appeared to strike each other "causing" various kinds of reactive movement. This impression of events as caused by "collisions" or "rebounds" was sometimes very strong, and by adapting and making use of certain Gestalt-type principles such as contiguity, proximity and good continuation Michotte was able to show how the perception of causality could be enhanced or reduced in ways that were predictable by the experimenter.

In conceptual terms it is not difficult to find parallels between Kelley's attempts to define the nature of social explanations in terms of his three-dimensional ANOVA model, and Michotte's much earlier work to find a similar interactive model to define the phenomenal experience of causality in the visual mode, using Gestalt principles.

Importantly, at roughly the same time as Michotte was working on phenomenal causality in the visual mode, Heider was doing similar work with a social import to it. In a study by Heider and Simmel (1944), subjects were presented with visual stimuli of the type illustrated below in Fig. 1.

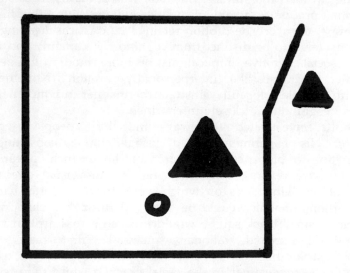

Fig. 1. Stimulus of the type used in the Heider studies

In the example given, the small circle moved around inside the square, followed closely by the large triangle. From time to time the small circle bumped against the sides of the square. Subsequently, the small triangle (outside the square) moved into contact with the top right-hand side of the square, and after a brief pause moved away again. At this point, the upper section of the right-hand side of the square opened, making a gap in the perimeter as shown in the figure. The small circle then went through the gap so created.

When viewing stimuli of this type, subjects who were asked to describe what was happening gave explanations which were causal, and which ascribed *social* motives and intentions to the objects. The circle was the heroine, pursued by the wicked villain (large triangle) from whom she was trying to escape. Subsequently, the hero (small triangle) saved the heroine by opening the door for her.

The reason for taking a step backwards to the work of Michotte and Heider in the 1940's is simple. In the examples cited above, the stimuli consisted of nothing more than moving drawings of meaningless objects (meaningless in the sense of having no particular referent) in a purely visual display. There were no physical collisions, no rebounds, no people, no pursuits, no villains or heroines and so forth. None the less, when viewing such stimuli, people produced causal accounts in the physical domain (action/ reaction) and in the social domain (pursuit, escape, rescue). These facts can be summarised simply by saying that *people regularly and predictably see patterns of causality where such causality does not exist.* Alternatively, if we wish to avoid the philosophical criticism that phenomenal causality is the only type of causality there is (Hume 1739-40), we would have to qualify this by saying that people regularly see physical and social causality in circumstances where a 'scientific' account would ascribe no such relationships.

Deriving from the above paragraph, we now see that there is great scope for confusion when people view objects that 'really do' knock each other over, or people who 'really do' chase each other about. In the early work of Michotte and Heider we have little difficulty in realising that the causal accounts provided are primarily psychological constructions, rather than accounts of scientific causality; mainly because we can see that the stimuli do not actually warrant the latter type of description. Squares and triangles, for example, cannot have motives and intentions.

Suppose however that the identical causal account derives from circumstances in which real objects or real people are involved. The tendency in this instance is to see the causal account as in some sense 'real', simply because such an account is possible given (our knowledge of) the nature of the situation, which is coincidentally 'real'. Consequently, the explanation offered looks feasible or appropriate in these circumstances. In fact however, the causal account may be identical to, and constructed from the same elements as, that produced in response to artificial stimuli. Viewing 'the real thing' does not invoke a different explanatory process, nor does it guarantee a different or more 'true' type of explanation. We have to conclude therefore that the 'truth' of a causal account cannot be inferred from looking at the circumstances surrounding it, although it's salient features may well be predictable from those circumstances.

It is worth stressing that, given the quasi-logical nature of the psychological processes involved, most such accounts will probably seem eminently plausible in an appropriate context, without this in any way attesting to the veridical value of the account; and different people possessing different knowledge will produce different but equally plausible accounts. For example, explanations of 'why people use drugs' given by drug users may differ from explanations given by non-drug users. Furthermore, as we shall see in a later chapter, features of drug users explanations may well be predictable from knowledge of the extent and pattern of their drug use. However, their explanations cannot be assumed to be qualitatively different from other people's explanations, or to be more 'true', simply by virtue of the fact that drug use is for them 'real'. Least of all is there any reason to presume that their causal accounts of drug use are scientific where other people's are social constructions.

As both Michotte and Kelley have implied, causal accounts are constructed according to certain rules which have no bearing on whether the account is ultimately veridical or not. This principal remains intact, even if we argue with Michotte or Kelley about the precise components they use in their respective models. Accordingly, within the constraints of a particular phenomenon, the investigation of people's causal accounts of that phenomenon has nothing in principle to do with the investigation of its causality as conceptualised by 'science', and we cannot carelessly use the one as a means of investigating the other.

Extending the Framework of Attribution

So far, a picture of attribution theory has been presented which seeks to point out various differing approaches to the psychological study of social explanation. Rather than being a single entity, attribution theory is more a group of theories held together by a common agenda within which coherent strands may be discerned. However, the account is so far limited in two ways.

Firstly, there are clearly a number of possible solutions to the problem of deciding what the most important dimensions of attribution are. One does not have to accept Kelley's, or anyone elses, dimensions as definitive since the basic principle of quasi-logical inference remains unaltered even if changes are made to the components. Second and more important, however, is the fact that classical attribution theory concentrates on the ways in which the inference process works; that is, on the manner in which people derive their explanations. The problem of how those explanations might relate to present or future actions has remained unaddressed until more recently, and it is to these two issues that we now turn.

2

Attribution Theory and Attributional Research

The bulk of research into attribution theory has used changes in type of explanation as the dependent variable; that is, investigations have concentrated on the ways in which differences or changes in people's explanations occur as a consequence of varying something else. For example, in a typical study the experimenter will describe some situation to his/her subjects. Then, by varying the information on (for example) consensus, consistency or distinctiveness, he/she will examine the ways in which the type of explanation offered varies as a consequence.

In contrast the extent to which attributions might predict a) present and b) future behaviour has been investigated less often, and perhaps with more equivocal success. Unfortunately, it is just this latter connection which is of the greatest potential interest from an applied or clinical perspective. There is much interest in the clinical field in cognitive/behavioural therapies which include techniques based on 'misattribution' and 'reattribution', even though the nature of the relationship between attributions and behaviour remains under-researched and to some extent philosophically problematic. The central idea is that by encouraging clients to explain their difficulties in new ways, and to abandon old and unhelpful modes of explanation, their *behaviour* will ultimately change in a manner which is beneficial. However, this apparently simple idea gives rise to a minefield of intertwined psychological, philosophical, existential and ethical problems, some of which are summarised in Totman (1982). Within this context, the following statement from Brewin and Antaki (1982) is extremely telling;

'. . .the usefulness of the various aetiological models employed by psychotherapists lies not in their truth or falsity, but in the ease with which they help clients to reattribute their problems in the desired direction. . . . .'

What this appears to mean, basically, is that it doesn't much matter whether the theory one produces to explain one's client's behaviour is 'true' or not, so long as it promotes a beneficial reappraisal; a conclusion which is highly insightful and, one suspects, 'true'. But it also implies a degree of theoretical catch-as-catch-can at a surface level that some psychologists might find difficult to live with. It implies that the patient's problem is frequently understood by neither the client nor the therapist; worse, the therapist appears to have a choice between self-delusion and client deception.

The quote from Brewin and Antaki (*op cit*) also poses some practical and ethical questions. It could mean, for example, that telling alcoholics that they are suffering from a disease is a useful thing to do if it enables them to stay sober, even if the disease notion is of doubtful validity; a point specifically raised by Cook (1988) in a review of the Minnesota treatment regime when he writes:

'There are many criticisms of the validity of the disease concept of alcoholism. . . . . However, the benefits described are real enough even if it is theoretically invalid.' (p.743).

However, knowingly providing 'invalid' information to clients to the effect that they are suffering from an illness, in the interests of attaining a particular treatment goal, is the first step on a slippery slope. For example, it might conceivably be beneficial in terms of the therapist's goals (if not the client's) to tell certain depressed and inward-looking patients that they have terminal cancer and only eighteen months to live, if this changed their cognitive/motivational state and made them behave in a more purposive and dynamic fashion; but the 'treatment' would not be without negative side effects, of which stress would be just one. Similarly, telling people they have the 'disease' of alcoholism might also be expected to have negative side effects even if it sometimes enables them to control their drinking.

The inventor of the Derailleur Gear, the device used to change gear on racing cycles and which defies most of the established rules of good engineering practice, remarked 'C'est brutale; mais ca marche.' He might also have pointed out that the system places unusual stresses on the component parts, which distort and wear out more quickly as a result. 'C'est brutale; mais ca marche' may be an apt epithet for addiction therapies which explain clients problems in terms of a disease, where such explanation is believed to change behaviour, rather than believed to be true. If as suggested by Cook (*op cit*) the approach has benefits which are 'real enough', the stresses and distortions are also frequently plain to see.

Most of the major issues involved in applying the attributional approach within the clinical setting have been sensitively discussed in Brewin and Antaki (*op cit*) and in Totman (*op cit*). It is clear that the cost-benefit payoff between aetiological statements of unknown validity, and the possibility of client behaviour change, has to be examined on a case-by-case basis. However, even if the use of attributional principles in the therapeutic setting poses both logical and ethical questions, attributional-behavioural links have been found to exist in other contexts.

In a review by Kelley and Michela (1980) a general model of the attribution field is proposed which distinguishes between attribution theories and attribution*al* theories. The former category refers to classic research which attempts to describe the circumstances under which people adopt various types of explanations, whilst the latter looks for links between attributions and behavioural consequences. Furthermore, there is an implication that the latter is viewed by the purists as *mere* attributional research. In Kelley and Michela's schematic model, for example (a version of which is presented in Fig.2 below), the arrows and link-lines connecting the third, and for all practical purposes, crucial box to the rest of the model are drawn in thin lines by those authors, in contrast to the bold lines linking the first two parts of the model. According to Eiser (1983) this represents the *de facto* situation that most research looks at the links between the first two boxes; but he also suggests that this represents Kelley and Michela's 'own implicit view of the 'proper' scope of attribution theory'.

Eiser argues however for the opposite point of view, suggesting that whilst the study of social perception as an end in itself is perfectly valid, the possible predictive implications of attributional research are in principle of the utmost significance in an applied sense. This is true even if such prediction is in the first instance merely associational rather than future-predictive. Eiser also goes

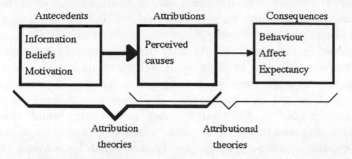

Fig. 2. The Kelley and Michela model.

on to point out the difficulties which remain to be overcome in the area of attributional research, whenever cognitions are seen as causal agents *vis a vis* behaviour. Nonetheless, by highlighting the attribu*tional* aspects of attribution as an area of potentially major importance, Eiser lays the foundations for an examination of the notion of *addiction* from an attributional standpoint. His own studies showing relationships in the real world between aspects of smoking behaviour and smokers attributions for their smoking, are described later in the text and serve as a model for much of what is to come.

The implications of a well-founded body of attributional research are in principle very far-reaching. It would be useful, for example, to know if the explanation of heavy regular drug use in terms of 'addiction' and all that is implied by that term, has its basis in attribution, rather than being scientifically derived, and evidence will be presented on this in a later chapter. However, once this is established, the possibility arises that such beliefs might have attributional implications for drug-taking behaviour. In other words, the very act of explaining drug use in certain habitual ways might help to maintain and develop a drug problem in those terms.

However, we are again in danger of proceeding too rapidly to a conclusion, and it is necessary to step back once more and examine certain other evidence which does not fit within the classic attribution mould. Amongst a number of alternative approaches to attribution, the work of Weiner deserves special attention. In a number of publications, Weiner makes significant contributions to the nuts-and-bolts of attributional explanation, by postulating dimensions which differ fundamentally from those offered by Kelley ; and which also seem better suited to the task of developing attributional theories.

Weiner's attributional approach stems from studies of achievement motivation, and his attributional model of 'achievement-related behaviour' (Weiner *et al* 1971; Weiner 1974) is well summarised in Bar-Tal (1982). Weiner based many of his studies on school-pupils' success or failure in school-related tasks like examinations or tests, but in principle the theory generalises to success and failure in other areas. The theory is basically a two-stage one involving both attribution and attributional theory. Firstly, he observes that people make reference to a variety of causes when explaining their success or failure on achievement tasks; explanations which arise in the manner of attributions as described previously. However, what gives Weiner's work its distinctive attributional flavour is his insistence that the nature of this explanation has important consequences for the persons cognitive, affective and behavioural reactions. For example, poor performance perceived as due to 'having a bad cold on the day' does not preclude success next time; whereas poor performance perceived as 'due to lack of basic ability' suggests that future attempts will also meet with failure. Proceeding further, the former explanation serves as a basis for continued effort, whereas the latter holds out little hope and may be taken as a justification for quitting.

In a series of studies Weiner produced evidence of associations between type of explanation and behaviour, persistence and quitting being only two of the variables studied which showed relationships with style of explanation for success or failure (see Bar-Tal *op cit*). However, in illustrating these attributional relationships Weiner employed a set of dimensions which have subsequently proved useful within a number of applied contexts but which differ from those of Kelley. Whilst some of Weiner's work involves up to five dimensions, three of these have proved to be the most powerful and have been more widely employed than any others. These form the central basis for the Weiner model. They are:

a) *locus* – is the cause of the behaviour seen as originating within the person (i.e. drive, energy, ability, enthusiasm, effort etc), or within the environment? (family, friends, opportunity, 'background' etc). If the former, the locus is said to be *internal*; if the latter, *external*.

b) *stability* – is the cause of the behaviour seen as fluctuating and variable over time (i.e. a cold, luck, the weather, a chance meeting etc) or is it a permanent feature? (non-curable illness, enduring family situation, nationality, etc.) If the former, the perceived cause is *unstable*; if the latter, *stable*.

c) *controllability* – is the cause seen as under the volitional control of the individual (effort, obtaining resources, making friends) or as outwith that control? (task difficulty, victimisation, lack of opportunity etc.) If the former, the cause is seen as *controllable*; if the latter, *uncontrollable*.

It will be apparent that these dimensions are also interactive, and that most of the examples given above can be coded in terms of two, or all three, of Weiner's dimensions. For example, effort is both unstable and internal; task difficulty is both external and unstable. In addition, there is a logical problem insofar as controllability appears to be redundant in some situations, since it is implicit in certain stable/internal combinations. Yet in many circumstances it appears to have a life of its own, making a further contribution to prediction. For example, drug use seen as due to external, stable factors (e.g. bad social and economic circumstances) *ought* to be uncontrollable; but people do not always see it that way.

Weiner's dimensions, and particularly the interaction of stability with locus, have proved helpful in the investigation of attributions in a number of areas including health, illness and addiction. This is because Weiner's system is better suited to the task of classifying or categorising attributions, whereas Kelley's system is primarily suited to the task of classifying the behaviours from which attributions derive. In other words, Weiner's is basically an attribution*al* typology.

Locus of Control and Cognitive Style

When considering Heider's contribution to attribution theory, it was found helpful to refer to earlier investigations into the perception of causality by Michotte. Following a parallel course, it is now worthwhile tracing the roots of attributional research back to some earlier concepts. The idea of locus (the internal/external dimension) is not an original contribution from Weiner, but is derived in the first instance from Rotter's notion of 'locus of control'. The basic reference to Rotter is a 1966 paper in which the locus of control concept was postulated and in which Rotter's I-E (internal/external) scale was described; a scale which measured the dimension internal/external. The locus of control concept attempted to classify people according to the extent to which they felt able to control or influence things that happened to them, and the I-E scale conceptualised this trait as a quasi-personality dimension which could be measured. According to the theory, people high in internality would believe that their actions could influence events; for example, that voting is a useful way of shaping the nature of government; or that joining Greenpeace is a useful way of combating global pollution; or that recovery from an illness depends on personal effort, and so forth. On the other hand, a high external person would believe that voting was a waste of time; that Greenpeace makes no difference since decisions are made by people in high office without regard to public opinion; or that recovery from an illness depends on the treatment.

As will be reported in later chapters, attempts to distinguish between people with alcohol, smoking or drug problems and those with no such problems, in terms of I-E scores, have produced ambiguous and sometimes contradictory results, but the fact that the attempt was made is interesting. As far as addiction problems are concerned, the implication of the I-E dimension is that people who are high on internality will feel able to control their substance use, and will thus be more likely to succeed in doing so; whereas those who are high external will feel unable to do so and will consequently behave like 'addicts'. However, such a clear picture has never emerged. Whilst a number of studies have shown 'locus of control' to be an element which has predictive value when used in conjunction with other variables, especially in the area of health and various forms of the Health Belief Model (see for example King 1983), Rotter's dimension by itself has made a somewhat ambiguous contribution to the understanding of addiction.

On the other hand, Weiner's model which makes use of a very similar 'locus' concept has produced more consistent results, and it is instructive to examine why this might be. The most obvious explanation is that Weiner's basic model uses three dimensions where Rotter uses only one. However, this is an oversimplification. The fact is that Rotter's formulation actually involves *all three* dimensions but does not permit their independent manipulation. The title 'locus of control' confounds locus with controllability from the outset; and the fact that Rotter produced a scale to measure the I-E dimension indicates that he assumed the dimension to have stability over time and across situations i.e. to be a trait.

Consequently, 'locus of control' contains all the elements of Weiner's three-component model, but in a form that makes them individually inaccessible.

The idea that 'locus of control' might have some consistency, even to the point of being considered a quasi-personality dimension, raises a further issue. In the first chapter, we found a clear analogy between perception of causality in the visual and social domains when considering the work of Michotte and of Heider. In a similar way, there is a connection between Rotter's 'locus of control' and earlier work by Witkin, again in the area of perception.

Witkin's Studies of Field Dependence

Witkin was concerned with the perception of *verticality* in a number of experiments carried out in the late 1940's (Witkin and Asch, 1948a, 1948b; Asch and Witkin, 1948a, 1948b). In the studies by Witkin and Asch, subjects were seated in a completely dark room, and presented with a visual array. The stimulus, known as the 'rod and frame', consisted of a luminous square frame, inside which was a single luminous line or 'rod'. Both the frame and the rod were pivoted on shafts attached to their centres, enabling them to be tilted one way or the other independently. The darkness of the room precluded subjects from seeing anything other than the luminous rod and frame. In a series of experiments, the frame-part of the visual array was tilted one way or the other by measured amounts; after which the subject was asked to set the rod to the true vertical. Many elaborations to this basic method were evolved, including a condition in which the rod, the frame, and the position of the subject, could all be tilted one way or the other. The basic data consisted of measuring how accurately subjects could locate true vertical under the various conditions. Describing some of their findings, Witkin and Asch (1948b) wrote:

> 'Although most S's, even when influenced by the frame, were able to make judgments without undue trouble, some encountered very serious difficulty. The latter kind of performance, obtained solely with S's who were greatly influenced by the frame, was characterised by marked confusion, prolonged effort in reaching a decision, very large errors, and in extreme cases an utter inability to establish the upright.' (from Vernon, 1966, p.142).

The idea of 'troubled' performance in the above studies led to the notion that people varied along a continuum from *field dependent* to *field independent*; and furthermore, by examining the correlation between subjects' performance on different tasks in different studies, which proved to be substantial and significant, Witkin and Asch were led to conclude that 'a given degree of dependence on the visual framework tends to characterise a person's perception in a fairly general way.' In other words, a field-dependent or field-independent perceptual 'style' might be a stable characteristic of individuals i.e. a 'perceptual trait'.

The reader will realise that the idea of a field-dependent or independent style in the domain of visual perception is analogous to the notion of internal or external locus as suggested by Rotter in the field of social perception. Whereas the I-E dimension classifies behavioural outcomes according to whether they are explained in terms of factors internal to, or outwith, the control of the individual, the field-dependence/independence notion classifies perception in terms of the influence of an internal standard as opposed to an external frame of reference.

At one time, there was much interest in the possibility that field-dependence/independence might be part of a general cognitive style which crossed a number of perceptual/cognitive boundaries; and within that context the inclusion of Rotter's I-E dimension as a measure of 'social field dependence' would have seemed a natural step to take. For example, in addition to the rod-and-frame test, the notion of Cognitive Style also came to include performance on such tasks as Embedded Figures, Stroop Test, Critical Flicker Fusion, Phi-phenomenon and Einstellung. Furthermore, correlations between performance on such tasks and certain personality measures led some workers to conclude that they in fact measured stable personality traits in a more general sense. For example, Pemberton (1952) suggested that performance on the Embedded Figures test was associated with self-centredness or nonconformity; and whilst these data are not strong, one can see *ex post facto* how internality/externality and field dependence/independence might both relate to such things as self-centredness and non-conformity. In a similar way, MacArthur (1955) referred to a common factor derived from a variety of tests as 'social suggestibility in situations demanding persistence' (from Cronbach, 1960, p.556) clearly implying some sort of 'social field dependence.'

However, despite the obvious attraction of placing locus of

control firmly in the realm of cognitive style, Witkin and Goodenough expressly deny that they make appropriate bedfellows. They write in a footnote, (Witkin and Goodenough 1981; p.48):

'The field-dependence-independence construct is conceptually quite different from other constructs to which they bear a surface similarity. One of these is locus of control.'

Witkin then cites three studies showing low associations between the two, before concluding, 'Whereas field-dependence-independence is a process variable. . . .. . .locus of control is an attitudinal or belief variable.'

Despite these assertions, however, there are reasons for thinking that Witkin may not in fact have the last word on the issue. We have already commented on the fact that Rotter's concept generally fails to perform as well as it might, due to the fact that it is factorially complex, so it's failure to correlate highly with measures of cognitive style might to some extent be anticipated on those grounds. Furthermore, Witkins' categorical separation of process and attitudinal variables appears somewhat out of step with contemporary thinking on social cognition, where the interaction of perceptual and cognitive factors is generally given much greater prominence. Nonetheless, despite his express denial in this specific instance, Witkin clearly saw important and extensive ramifications for social behaviour within the domain of cognitive style, devoting an entire section to this train of thought in his classic monograph (*op cit*). He writes (p39):

'Further evidence that people who are field independent in perception of the upright also function more autonomously in their interpersonal relationships comes from the repeated characterisation of them by others as being high in autonomy and as showing initiative, responsibility-taking, self-reliance, and the ability to think for themselves,' and later (p43) '. . . .people who are field dependent in perception of the upright and limited in disembedding ability have an interpersonal orientation, whereas people who are field independent and competent in disembedding have an impersonal orientation. Thus, the former kinds of people, more than the latter, pay selective attention to social cues; they favour situations that bring them into contact with others over solitary situations; they prefer educational-vocational domains that are social in content and require working with people; they seek physical closeness to people in their social interactions; and they are more open in their feelings.'

These, and many other examples from his work, reveal that Witkin clearly saw implications from his studies of perception of the upright, for social behaviours in a wide range of domains.

Inadequacy Explanations of Drug Use

The idea of a continuity between perceptual, cognitive and social/ behavioural 'styles' is an issue that has fascinated many researchers; and it can be argued that in a general sense Rotter's ideas do not look obviously out of place in such company. The basic idea behind Cognitive Style was that, given that 'the organism is an information processing system, simple perceptual tests may identify its constant characteristics' (Cronbach *op cit* 1960). With respect to addiction, it is easy to see how problem drinking or problem drug use might be seen as deriving from a generalised trait of social field dependence, the inability of the sufferer to 'disembed' his/her own consumption behaviour from the behaviour of others, coupled to the kind of social/interpersonal orientation suggested by Witkin *et al.* This is very close to some of the more trite theories based on peer-group pressure or other forms of social influence, which conceptualise the drug user as a naive innocent led astray by others because he/she is unable to withstand the pressures exerted by particular contexts; rather like the field-dependent subjects in Witkin's studies.

In fact, the failure of drug-studies to show clear relationships between aspects of cognitive style such as field-dependence, or locus of control, probably indicates a fundamental flaw in our thinking about addiction, rather than a simple methodological problem. 'Inadequacy models' of drug use, conceptualising the problem as one of naive innocents subverted by others as a consequence of personal weakness and the inability to resist outside pressures, are outdated and unhelpful. Such models are comforting in the short term, since they imply that normal or adequate people do not take drugs. But the explanation overlooks some basic truths such as the fact that taking drugs is pleasurable, and that by and large people who take drugs do so because they want to and because they like it, rather than because they are forced into it by outside pressures. Furthermore, most of them are probably not trying to stop, and most of them are not experiencing any major problems other than keeping it secret. It is clear that one does not have to be sick or inadequate to be curious about drugs, to want to try them, or to wish to use them for their positive effects from time to time. From such a viewpoint, there is no reason to expect drug users to be more field-dependent, or external, than anyone else.

Once we abandon 'inadequacy' explanations for drug use, opting instead for the view that people can and do use drugs for their own good (subjectively rational) reasons, both internal and external, stable and unstable in variable proportions, there is no reason to expect links between drug use and any general cognitive style or personality type. The point of this argument is not therefore to suggest that simple and straightforward links exist between 'locus' or 'field-dependence' and drug use, but rather the opposite. Furthermore, *because* there is little evidence for a link between drug use and any general cognitive style, any consensus which emerges with some regularity in particular kinds of context (for example, stable/internal or 'helpless addict' explanations for drug use given by clients in the clinical or counselling context) must derive primarily from that context, and be produced by that context. Most importantly, if such a context does lead to an attributional consensus, which it appears in fact to do, then the preceding paragraphs on the attributional properties of explanation suggest a mechanism whereby subsequent behaviour can be adversely affected. In other words, the more we treat drug problems as if they were the domain of inadequate, sick or helpless people, the more people will present themselves within that framework, and the more we will produce and encounter drug users who fit that description.

Furthermore, at a theoretical level we can no longer easily dismiss the attributional link as merely attribution theory's poor relation. The pedigree of attributional research is in many ways comparable with that of the classic attribution approach, and indeed has many elements which bear a striking cross-resemblance including a basis in early studies of perception (Michotte and Witkin) and an interim period linking early ideas to later studies of social-cognition (Heider and Rotter). For these reasons, we have to disagree with Kelley and Michela that in some sense attributional research is a less important or more speculative field of study, and argue instead that a full examination of the role of attributions requires a recognition of the equal status of attributional research, and an integration of the two strands.

3

Volitional and Non-Volitional Explanations

In the previous chapters the bases for attribution theory were reviewed from two points of view. First, we reviewed the body of research and theory which links the kinds of explanations people offer to their observations of, or knowledge about, the situation to be explained. The easiest model to understand is that proposed by Kelley, and this was covered in basic detail. Secondly, we reviewed the evidence which seeks to show links between attributions and subsequent behaviour and here the work of Weiner featured prominently.

It was pointed out that from the attribution theory perspective, the predictions of the theory concern the *type* of explanation that will be produced in given circumstances, but say nothing about the validity of that explanation. In other words, the emphasis is on the internal logic of the explanation process, rather than the product. From the attributional perspective, a number of possible attribution-to-behaviour links were discussed, and several studies were cited to demonstrate such links. Consequently, there is sufficient evidence to permit the postulation of a route whereby explanations which are not true might nonetheless influence human action; exactly the point made by Heider (*op cit*).

The main point this book wishes to develop is that conceptualising drug use in terms of 'addiction' is primarily an illustration of how attribution works, rather than being a 'true' or 'scientific' account. Furthermore, such a conception has attributional implications for the behaviour of those concerned, including drug-takers, treatment specialists, educators, legislators and many others.

However, before developing this point in detail, there is one more aspect of attribution which must be addressed, namely the functional nature of certain types of explanation in particular situations.

When discussing Kelley's model (*op cit*) the point was made that it was not necessary for an observer to have direct, multiple observations in order to arrive at an explanation. The literature refers to the involvement of 'causal schemata' in the instance where there is incomplete information; but there is no reason in principle why widely held prior beliefs, expectancies, attitudes, stereotypes and other aspects of subjective social knowledge might not reliably and regularly substitute for direct observations, even though the inclusion of such variables goes way beyond what the classic attribution theorists intend. However, to the extent that an explanation is produced which is primarily congruent with social cognitions rather than with direct observations, we may speak of *preferred* and *non-preferred* explanations. For instance, the examples given in the opening chapter of politicians' explanations for popular, as opposed to unpopular, policy decisions, are really illustrations of preferred forms of explanation deriving in a limited way from perceptions and in a major way from social cognitions. It is clear that particular types of explanation can be primarily *functional*; their main purpose is not to explain in any scientific sense, but to justify an action, to reduce culpability, to attract praise, to make sense of a situation and so forth. There is an extensive literature on self-serving bias in attributions which goes some way towards illustrating this point, and self-serving and other forms of bias are discussed in a later chapter.

In other words, the further we move from the situation of direct observations, the less any given explanation is derived in the manner of the naive scientist, on the basis of what is perceived; and the more the explanation derives from things that the explainer brings to the situation at the outset, in the form of longer-term social cognitions. 'Addiction', it is argued, is primarily an explanation derived according to the principles of attribution theory, rather than the principles of 'science' as normally conceptualised; and it has its basis primarily in certain stereotyped cognitions concerning drugs and drug users, and only to a limited degree in direct observations of drugs and drug users going about their normal business. As such it is primarily a functional, or 'preferred' form of explanation.

The Preference for External Explanations

It is clear that socially functional or preferred forms of explanation are regular features of social interaction and as such are commonplace. Further examples will be described later in the text. However, the preference for explanations in terms of external rather than internal factors is of special concern since such a preference lies at the heart of one of the most influential of 'scientific' psychological theories of recent times, namely the operant psychology of B.F.Skinner; a psychology which epitomises the 'scientific' approach for many practitioners. Basically, Skinner placed the control of human behaviour in the environment, a position from which he never wavered. On the other hand, at different times he viewed the contribution of the organism in a more variable fashion, ranging from the denial of internal processes as having any significance, to the acceptance of thoughts and feelings as epiphenomena, through to their role as a source of reinforcement derived from the organism's learning history.

A major claim to usefulness of any scientific theory is that it makes possible the understanding and control of some phenomenon in a manner that is not possible through animistic types of explanation. However, whilst such is undeniably the case in the natural sciences, the usefulness of this approach when applied to human action is less certain. It is not immediately apparent that saying a piece of behaviour is forced by environmental conditions invariably leads to better or more productive outcomes than saying that the person did this thing because he/she wanted to.

Saying that a rock falls downwards because it 'wants' to is animistic in a way that saying a person 'wants something' is not. People's 'wanting' has a physiological basis existing as processes inside the person, whereas no such processes are observed inside the stone. Consequently, to apply the same external explanatory framework to falling stones and behaving people is an act of choice, the choice being to ignore the fact that events take place inside the person that do not take place inside the stone; events which might merit some independent consideration. To the extent that this is true, Skinner's is not a scientific theory; rather, it represents an act of choice. Namely, the choice to proceed as if stones and people were the same in having no internal processes on which to base a causal phenomenology, even though observation shows that this is not in fact the case. In other words, the explanation of human behaviour in terms of external loci has more in common with preferred forms of explanation (i.e. functional attribution) than with what we normally expect of a scientific account.

Unfortunately, the explanation of human action by reference to external factors has come to be viewed in some circles as the only legitimate route to a scientific understanding of human behaviour. It should be clear, however, that to ignore internal events and proceed is if they did not occur or had no significance is an act of choice rather than an act of science. Furthermore, such internal events are not magical, and we do not have to resort to metaphysics or 'the soul' in order to sustain this argument. These internal events can be explained in principle (if not in fact) in terms of the same logical-positivist philosophy that we apply to external events; but we cannot claim to be more scientific by virtue of having ignored them or ruled them out of court. It begins to look as if a scientific account in terms of levers and flashing lights might be preferred to a scientific account of motives and intentions simply because it is easier.

The Behaviourist Approach of B.F.Skinner

A scientific account of behaviour can hardly overlook the fact that people, animals, trees, flowers, and living things generally, are biological mechanisms and the nature of the mechanisms involved has a determining influence on the repertoire of behaviours available to each. However, a mechanistic explanation at a given micro-level is inadequate to account for the molar actions of people and animals insofar as it fails to take account of the different-level mechanisms of consciousness, reasoning, decision-making, and other loosely-defined but important processes that result in a given environment being interpreted differently by different individuals. To put this another way, whilst at a given level there are clear similarities in biological/physiological functioning between species members, the fact that members of the same class will frequently show different behaviours in the same circumstances means that, from a logical-positivist perspective, there must be non-common events taking place at some second level. We can call this second level consciousness or decision-making; or describe it in terms of differences in neural transmission at some specified site, as we wish, without altering the central argument. An explanation at a given level is not an explanation at any other level.

People, and animals too, do not respond to a common environment, but rather (in phenomenological terms) they respond to what they as individuals feel the implications and properties of that environment are. An explanation of the mechanisms underlying an emitted piece of behaviour is thus not a total account; least of all an explanation of why that piece of behaviour was chosen in the first place. The physiology of walking does not explain why people walk down the street; and people walk down the street because they have reasons for so doing which derive from a physiology/pharmacology totally unrelated to the physiology of walking. With respect to addiction, mechanism is commonly assumed to be based on drug pharmacology, but in fact it cannot be simply assumed that the pharmacology of drug action is the same as the pharmacology of deciding to use, or not to use, drugs.

Nor can the observation that a person keeps performing some act over and over again cannot be used to infer that the person therefore *has to* do it, or that they cannot stop; least of all that non-volitional mechanisms of behaviour have supplanted mechanisms of mind or choice. More importantly, a logical-positivist perspective requires that all behaviour shall ultimately have a physicalistic basis. From such a standpoint, one cannot conclude that drug-related behaviour is 'less free' than other behaviour, since the viewpoint does not permit differences in that dimension. The non-drug-user is forced *not* to use just as much as the user is forced to use; and consequently an explanation in terms of differences in volition is untenable within that 'scientific' context.

Despite the logical wreckage created by the collision of scientific and phenomenological accounts in such areas as addicted behaviour, mind-free explanations have a long and pervasive history and continue to exert a powerful influence on the way we think about certain problems notwithstanding more recent developments in cognitive psychology. Skinner's ideas are particularly attractive and compelling, and we shall use them to illustrate a certain approach, an approach which permeates thinking on a far broader front. Basically, he 'solved' the mind/behaviour problem by denying that there was any such problem. According to the Skinnerian view, experience, choice and decision-making are merely past reinforcement history, and the entire realm of human thought is basically an epiphenomenon, a by-product of the operation of inferred but unspecified mechanisms (Skinner, B.F. 1973; 1974). The implication is that if certain environmental features are correctly controlled, people will automatically behave in certain ways. What they think about it is an irrelevance, and the idea that they behave in that way because they choose to do so is an absurdity. The rat in the Skinner box is assumed to press the lever because it has to, rather than because it chooses to do so or feels there is no reasonable alternative under the circumstances, and people are assumed to operate in basically the same way.

Skinner's explanation of behaviour was centred totally on external environmental factors, but the fallacy of the single-level mechanistic account can be repeated at any level. With drugs for example, the single-level mechanistic account is based on the pharmacology of drug action. Once it has been established that a drug has a measurable pharmacological effect on someone, it is a short but supremely illogical step to assume that 'therefore' the person has no further decision making capacity. It is simply assumed that drug pharmacology has wiped out and replaced the pharmacology of choice behaviour. From here, we can easily arrive at an absurd conceptualisation of addiction implying that a person can engage in a coherent and carefully-planned sequence of actions such as getting out of bed, phoning a taxi, going into town, stealing a coat from a shop, selling the coat, and finally keeping a rendezvous with an acquaintance who has spare heroin to sell, because he/she *has to*; whilst all the time he/she is desperately trying not to do any of these things. The pharmacology of drug action is assumed to compel the behaviour irrespective of, or against, the person's 'will'.

The position is complicated by the fact that a number of animal experimenters have succeeded in causing rats and monkeys to behave in highly self-destructive ways when under the influence of psychoactive substances; for example, creatures with cannulae inserted into parts of their brains, through which CNS stimulants can be delivered, have been found to press a lever for this type of self-gratification at the expense of eating, drinking and other activities essential to healthy living. In some studies, they have actually died in consequence. The issues surrounding these types of study will be dealt with in a later chapter, and it suffices for the time being to say that there are considerable problems in deciding exactly what is revealed by such studies. For the present, the point being made is purely a linguistic one, and concerns the way such behaviour is described. The finding that a rat, dosed on a CNS stimulant, will work continuously to get further doses becomes the occasion for the *ex post facto* suggestion that the rat 'has to' press the lever because it is 'addicted', rather than 'wants to' because it 'likes it'. In other words, the fact that stimulation of part of the brain is followed by a bout of incessant lever pressing, leads to the quite unwarranted conclusion that the owner of the brain (i.e. the sum total of the other mechanisms that make up the rest of this particular rat) has no say in the matter; and thence to a preference for an alternative type of account which serves functions which are social, rather than scientific. That is, it sounds 'scientific', and demonstrates that a 'scientist' 'understands' the behaviour in a way that the rest of us do not. In fact however, the relationship between the rat's behaviour and the environment is the important issue, and conceptualising that relationship entirely in terms of external pharmacological influences, as opposed to the interaction of internal *and* external factors, in no way develops our understanding of why people or animals take drugs. In fact, it hinders such an understanding.

Let us be quite blunt. Describing a behaviour as compelled merely on the basis of observations that it happens with great regularity is an act of superstition, and has nothing whatsoever in common with normal processes of scientific deduction. Furthermore the switch from a volitional view of behaviour to a mechanistic one is philosophically absurd. Thinking in areas of science where objects rather than sentient beings are involved has solved the animism problem several centuries ago, and scientific thought and animism now make strange bedfellows within Western conceptualisations of science. Within that conceptualisation, one cannot launch a putative 'scientific' account of behaviour whose main and most salient characteristic is the switch from an animistic to a determinist account of a piece of behaviour. Rightly or wrongly, the former cannot exist within that 'scientific' view of the world.

Within the permitted 'rules' of that world view the fact that the tides of the sea invariably come and go with a precise periodicity, does not permit the conclusion that they do so because they 'have to'; and the fact that the cuckoo in Spring sometimes arrives and sometimes it doesn't cannot be taken to demonstrate that it comes when it 'wants to'. In the same way, incessant lever pressing by a rat cannot be taken to indicate that it 'has to'; since by implication this means that less-constant activity is voluntary; that is, a lower rate of response indicates that the rat presses the lever even though it doesn't 'have to'. In summary, it seems likely that observing an animal which displays a constant and repeated series of actions, leads to a causal account in terms of compulsion or necessity as a result of *perceptual* processes of the type described by Michotte and Heider in their studies of perceived causality, rather than from any scientific logic. In other words, we say that the rat is 'addicted' simply because its behaviour *looks* mechanical.

The philosophical imponderables at the heart of Skinnerian thinking have been discussed in detail in Wann (1964), Wheeler (1973), and Machan (1974). Basically, as suggested above, mechanism and volition cannot be used simultaneously within the same explanation. We cannot imply that some people work according to volitional principles whilst others are operating according to the laws of mechanism, and one cannot hop between these modes of explanation according to preference or convenience, in order to serve the needs of the moment. They are alternative modes of explanation for the same thing. Yet for some reason we seem to prefer mechanistic explanations in certain circumstances. With respect to addiction, we want to know that addicts operate according to a set of principles that do not apply to the rest of us, and the primary purpose of the 'addiction' label is to provide for that need. The reasons why we prefer to account for addicted behaviour in terms of a mechanistic rather than a volitional model is the topic for the remainder of this text.

It is also argued, however, that conceptualising drug use in terms of the subjectively rational choices that people make from amongst a range of available options opens up new avenues for treatment and policy which are not available from the standpoint of pharmacological compulsion. From the standpoint advocated, the explanation of addiction poses no problem apart from the one that confronts us all every day; the explanation of why addicts take drugs is no different in principle from the explanation of why any of us do anything. Consequently, no special 'treatment' domain is required when tackling drug problems; we can take help and assistance from anywhere.

The Behaviourist Legacy

Skinner did in fact put himself before the mast by spelling out the societal implications of his theory, as he saw them, in such books as

Reflections on Behaviorism and Society (1978), *Beyond Freedom and Dignity* (1973 *op cit*) and the intriguing novel *Walden Two* (1948) in which he described an entire Utopian society based on the principles of operant conditioning. By 'behavioural engineering', a human society was produced (*Walden Two*) in which, basically, all human problems were solved; in a sense, whether people wanted them solving or not. So attractive and compelling were Skinner's ideas that a number of Walden-Two type communities actually sprang into being; the most long-lasting of these being the well-documented Twin Oaks community which sought to incorporate the main principles of Walden Two as far as possible, and where, on cold winter evenings, the children were regaled with readings from the Book itself as the commune members sat round the fire (Kinkade, 1973).

Twin Oaks, one must probably conclude, was never Walden Two. It remained more like a struggling commune than the urbane, technologically sophisticated and economically thriving world of Skinner's dream. Furthermore, many of the problems that arose seem with hindsight to be more helpfully described as arising from the opinions, beliefs and attitudes of individuals, rather than from difficult-to-specify or presumed environmental inadequacies, though there were clearly problems with both. Lastly, Kinkade's book contrasts markedly in style with Walden Two. It is warm, affectionate, emotional, and crammed with phenomenology in a way that Walden Two is not. It reveals a struggling group of people trying to come to terms with a philosophy that becomes progressively more remote and absurd.

Skinner's vision fails at the grand level for practical as well as philosophical reasons but it remains one of the great psychological visions. However, in the absence of the Utopia, we have been left with the charred and increasingly trivialised remains of his theory. Although behaviourism might retain some usefulness as a conceptual tool for tackling certain societal problems within the context of an integrated approach comprising other more politically-aware philosophies, the principles are most frequently applied piecemeal in isolated settings; for example in the clinical context where they take the concrete-minded and literal forms epitomised by aversion therapy and token economies; or in the animal behaviour laboratory where, being literally a mindless theory, it seems useful in accounting for the behaviour of animals placed in a variety of pointless and unnatural situations. The contrast between Skinner's dream of the perfect society, and some of the more grubby manifestations of applied behaviourism is simply stunning. Skinner's novel remains an enigma, having earned widespread plaudits from supporters of the humanist cause, whilst at the same time coming under close scrutiny from other quarters to determine whether it constituted an attack on civil rights.

Putting Skinner's intriguing novel to one side for the time being, however, the principle residue of Skinner's theory appears to consist firstly of a conviction that people and animals do things because of the operation of mechanism rather than by magic, which is a reasonable assumption; plus the belief that the only mechanism necessary is one that translates environment into behaviour in a direct way without the person or animal *requiring* any sense of 'why' or 'because', which seems rather improbable. Without such a phenomenological link it is hard to see why organisms should behave at all. For Skinner, however, behaviour equals environment plus some more-or-less common physiology which latter has little predictive or explanatory value (1974 *op cit*); but more importantly behaviour seems to be something that happens *to* people, rather than being done *by* them. *In a similar way, 'addiction' is not conceptualised as something that people do, so much as something that happens to them.*

The Legacy of the Skinner Box

The Skinner box, as is well known, is a box into which one puts a rat or a pigeon as a means of controlling the creature's access to something crucial to life, such as food or water. A principal function of the box is to present a lever to creatures who know nothing about levers, whilst ensuring that they have no contact with objects or situations with which they are familiar and which might therefore influence their performance in ways that make interpretation of their actions more difficult from a behaviourist perspective. This is called experimental control. In general terms, the primary aim of Skinner-box studies is to discover what animals will do to obtain the basic necessities of life under these unnatural conditions, and thereby to shed light on the principles underlying normal behaviour.

Pressing the lever will usually provide the occupant with a pellet of food or a drop of water, or some similar reinforcer. Skinner's major observation was that in these circumstances rats and pigeons pressed the lever; a fact which for most of us would attest to their basic rationality and common sense. Skinner's major conclusion however was that rats and pigeons did not press the lever because they felt hungry, and realised that this was a good way to stay alive given the somewhat unusual circumstances. He preferred instead to explain things totally in terms of the box, the lever, and the feeding schedule, whilst specifically excluding any interaction of these things with what for want of better terms may be described as the motives and intentions of the occupant. The control of behaviour was thus located solely in the box, and not at all in the rat or pigeon.

From an attributional standpoint, Skinner's preference for explaining behaviour in terms of the environment removes any suggestion that behaviour takes place for reasons residing in the 'actor' (animal, person etc) although the reasons for the behaviour are nonetheless known to the 'observer' (experimenter); however the nature and logical status of that knowledge must remain uncertain given the nature of Skinner's theory and the fact that it also applies, one assumes, to behaviourists. On the other hand, we may if we choose describe the Skinner box and its occupant in anarchical terms, taking the opposite attributional perspective; namely that of the actor rather than the observer. Maybe, for instance, the rat presses the lever sooner or later because it seems to be the only thing in the cage that affords any opportunities. Everything else is bolted to the floor, and the lever is the only thing that moves. Perhaps the rat makes conscious note of the fact that food pops out of a hole whenever he/she presses the lever, and decides that pressing it is therefore the only way to obtain something to eat in this unnatural and inhospitable situation. At least this explanation provides the rat with a reason for pressing the lever; the alternative appears to be a witless death by starvation. All things considered, therefore, pressing the lever seems the best thing to do *despite* the unpromising long-term prospects implied by the environment.

This type of explanation is totally unacceptable to any self-respecting Skinner-boxer, since it is 'unscientific' even though it makes perfect sense to anyone else. From a Skinnerian position, it has two shortcomings. First, it violates 'the law of parsimony', a principle that requires any explanation offered to be the simplest and least complicated explanation possible, consistent with accounting for the facts. Whilst this seems straightforward enough, however, it is not always clear which of two contrasting explanations is the most simple or economical. For example, explaining behaviour in terms of the environment without reference to internal processes might arguably be just about the most tortuous and misleading way of going about it, rather like trying to explain how the motor car works by reference to traffic lights rather than the internal combustion engine. Its second deficiency is more obvious; it removes the magic of scientific discovery from the 'functional analysis of behaviour', and makes it look like nothing so much as a blinding flash of the completely obvious (see for example Machan *op cit*).

Addiction as Skinner Box

Nothing and no-body can be particularly clever in a Skinner box. A person would probably behave in much the same way as the rat behaves, given the choices available. There are no reasonable or relevant alternatives to choose between, and hence no meaningful decisions to make; the box is specifically designed to remove the confounding influence of mind as far as possible. Small wonder that the ensuing line of argument bears with it the implication that the explanation of behaviour remains the province of the scientist whilst remaining a complete mystery to the objects of study, who have no access to, or need of, such information in order to behave. Any thought-like processes that might occur are epiphenomena; people do not actually think; they only think they do. However, since the behavioural psychologist knows all this, he/she is not even of this world, unless his/her musings on the matter are as purposeless and artefactual as everyone else's.

The notion of 'addiction' has much in common with a Skinner box. It suggests that people take drugs because some mechanism over which they have no control forces them to do so. It implies ultimately that the reasons for using a drug lie at a level beyond personal knowledge or control, and that the user does not have any reasons of his/her own that are worth mentioning. Drug-taking is seen as a function of outside forces; not of the person concerned. Addiction is therefore a conceptual Skinner box, into which drug users are put when they get into trouble. The rat's behaviour is a function of the box but not of the rat; and the addict's behaviour is a function of drugs but not of the drug-taker. Finally, the therapist knows the 'real' reasons why the addict takes the drugs, and any suggestions from the patient that he/she does it on purpose because he/she likes it can be dismissed as either ridiculous, or with a neat shift of level, as deliberately obstructive.

Addictions and Skinner-boxes have one other property in common. It is virtually impossible to get out once you have been put inside.

4
Addiction, Withdrawals and Craving

In 1976, Edwards and Gross provided a provisional description of an Alcohol Dependence Syndrome which differed markedly from previous conceptions of 'alcoholism as an entity.' It is instructive to summarise the three species of argument which led to the postulation of this syndrome, as outlined in Edwards (1977). Firstly, Edwards was impressed by alcohol consumption statistics which demonstrated that within populations the distribution of consumption was unimodal. The prevailing assumption till that time had been that consumption was bi-modal with 'alcoholics' forming their own second mode around some higher mean consumption level. This in turn suggested that 'alcoholism' was therefore experienced by a special group of people whose consumption was discontinuous from that of normal drinkers. According to Edwards, however, contemporary arguments concerning bi-modality versus uni-modality (see for example Davies 1982) overwhelmingly favoured the uni-modal view, and implied that 'alcoholics' were 'not a species standing on their own, but a segment of the population defined only by a cutting point on a continuum. The concept of alcoholism as an entity seems therefore to take a knock.'

Secondly, Edwards took heed of evidence from a number of surveys which investigated population drinking practices. These showed that people moved in and out of periods of troubled drinking behaviour, often without any outside intervention; consequently, people who were 'alcoholics' at one time frequently did not behave like 'alcoholics' some time later. In addition, Edwards noted that what constituted a drinking problem varied according to the social setting; what was seen as problem drinking by one person might be seen as normal in a different social or class setting. To some extent, the definition thus appeared to be arbitrary. Edwards concluded that any satisfactory definition would have to take such differences into account; and that troubled drinking did not reside in the individual but resulted from the interaction of the individual with his/her environment.

Thirdly, Edwards examined D.L.Davies' claims (1962, 1969a, 1969b) to have identified 'alcoholics' whose drinking had returned to normal levels. Such an outcome would be impossible within existing conceptions of 'alcoholism', since the 'disease' would inevitably reinstate itself should the 'alcoholic' return to any form of drinking. However, the idea 'once an alcoholic, always an alcoholic,' did not appear to hold according to D.L.Davies' data. Furthermore, Edwards referred in general terms to studies in which controlled drinking rather than abstinence had been the treatment goal, and to other studies showing the extent to which drinking was influenced by external factors such as environmental cues. It should be stated that the issue of controlled drinking amongst former alcoholics remains a fairly contentious issue in some circles, but Edwards' 1977 paper shows how his thinking was nonetheless influenced by this phenomenon.

After reviewing this evidence, Edwards wrote 'In the face of such a mass of evidence coming from at least three directions, to retain the notion of a specific syndrome of alcohol dependence might seem obdurate.'

Edwards then described an alternative syndrome, under the heading of the Alcohol Dependence Syndrome; a provisional description of which was first offered in Edwards and Gross (1976 *op cit*). The revised syndrome is an attempt to reconcile the conflicting evidence, and at the same time come up with a conception of alcohol dependence in which pharmacological, physiological, environmental, social, cognitive and phenomeno-logical (experiential) variables are all taken into account. The syndrome is thus more broadly based than traditional concepts based on 'alcoholism' and 'the alcoholic', and takes into account types of influence not considered by those non-interactive and mechanistic conceptions of alcoholism which the Alcohol Depen-dence Syndrome seeks to replace.

In the Alcohol Dependence Syndrome an attempt is made to bring together the various different ways of conceptualising alcohol dependence under a common banner; one of its specific aims being to produce a synthesis which will facilitate communication between those with differing perspectives. In the end, there is some disagreement about how successful this attempted integration has been. It can be argued that one problem with the Edwards and Gross syndrome is precisely that it can mean all things to all people, particularly since the empirical status of the variables said to comprise it differs rather widely, all the way from physiological indices of withdrawal, to verbal statements about subjective awareness of compulsion to drink.

Two of the most severe critics have been Heather and Robertson (1981, 1985) who argue that certain aspects of controlled drinking amongst 'alcoholics' (i.e. the ability of 'alcoholics' to successfully achieve the goal of returning to normal patterns of alcohol consumption) appear to contradict not merely earlier conceptions of 'alcoholism', but also conflict with certain central features of the Alcohol Dependence Syndrome itself. They suggest that the new syndrome is little more than the old 'disease' model in sheep's clothing.

Nonetheless, Edwards and Gross's proposition is important because it represents an attempt to address and resolve a number of problems arising from simplistic notions of alcoholism as a single entity. It remains a matter for concern therefore that simplistic notions about 'alcoholism', 'alcoholics' and 'disease' still prevail in some treatment agencies; and that the cautious and far-from-revolutionary propositions of Edwards and Gross still set a pace which is too hot for many people to follow.

The point now arises that the comments made by Edwards in the context of alcohol problems might logically apply, directly or in modified form, to addictions of other kinds. The mere fact of arguing that 'addiction' to alcohol is more differentiated and less monolithic than hitherto conceptualised, highlights a need to examine 'addiction' to other drugs from a similar standpoint. Unfortunately, due to the illegal status of illicit drug use and the clandestine nature of the activity, comparable data are somewhat scarcer, and their quality is sometimes even more variable. In particular, data are still lacking on various aspects of normative drug use in the community, aspects of drug use which hospital- and clinic-based studies frequently have difficulty in addressing. Whilst hospital and clinic studies shed light on the medical aspects of drug use after something has gone wrong, they are generally less successful in providing a picture of what we may describe as normal drug use. In a similar way, a clinic-based study of 'alcoholics' would provide only oblique and ambiguous insights into the nature of normal alcohol use in the community, and a view of the drinker based on the 'alcoholic' would be highly misleading. However, before proceeding to the next stage of the argument, it should also be conceded that there are problems with self-reports of both alcohol and drug consumption and such self-reports form the basis for most of the population studies which have been carried out. Basically, the validity of self-reports remains problematic with respect to the absolute consumption levels that people report; a problem which is discussed in more detail in Chapter 8. However, the ordinal characteristics of such data are generally fairly robust; consequently, such reports may be expected to provide some idea of the distribution of consumption in a population, even if the validity of the absolute levels reported remains less certain.

Notwithstanding the above reservations, each of the three arguments advanced by Edwards can now with some qualifications be taken to apply to addictions involving other drugs. For example, although distribution statistics for illicit drug use are somewhat thin on the ground, studies of the self-reports of drug-users provide no evidence for the postulation of bi-modality. On the contrary, the evidence from studies of young people (Plant *et al* 1985; Coggans *et al*, 1990 and 1991; Davies and Coggans, 1991) suggests that whilst experience with illicit drugs is fairly common (about one in five youngsters report having tried an illicit drug on at least one occasion) reports of use grow progressively less numerous as extent of use increases. In other words, the data from young people are certainly not compatible with a bi-modal theory, the normative evidence suggesting a uni-modal distribution with an extended upper tail; exactly what is described for alcohol consumption. Furthermore, despite the public perception of drug use as the prerogative of a specific 'junkie' group, evidence from surveys of old and young alike shows that drug use is not confined to a particular group, but is a regular occurrence in 'non-junkie' sections of the community. This is true not merely for Class B drugs like cannabis, but also for cocaine. Ongoing research by Ditton and the Scottish Cocaine Research Group (1990 unpublished) in the central belt of Scotland suggests that 61% of a 'snowballed' sample had college or university qualifications, and of these one third (21% of the total sample) had higher degrees or professional qualifications;

and comparable research by Cohen (1989,1990) in Amsterdam highlights the prevalence of cocaine use in non-deviant subcultures. Finally, if one includes the widespread prescribing of mood-altering pharmaceuticals within the community, then it is clear that considerable numbers of people, far removed from the stereotyped junkie, are dependent on their drug of preference. Whilst none of these studies amounts to a detailed analysis of the precise nature of the drug-use distribution at the population level, they nonetheless attest to the fact that no instantly identifiable subset of drug users appears to exist, even though a stereotype of the junkie clearly exists. Certainly there is sufficient evidence to suggest, like Edwards, that ' 'drug-addicts' are not a species standing on their own,' and that 'the concept of addiction as an entity seems therefore to take a knock.'

With respect to Edward's second argument, the evidence is stronger. The studies of Stimson and Oppenheimer (1982) have shown how individuals move into and out of heroin and other addictions without outside intervention. The difference between public stereotypes of drug use, and the realities of the situation have been commented on widely (see for example Finnigan 1988, 1996); and the idea that drug use does not reside in the individual but results from the interaction of the individual with his/her environment seems so uncontroversial as to merit little further comment, given the wealth of evidence showing associations between drug use, attitudes and values, and social and economic circumstances (see for example Dorn and South 1987; also the critique of Dorn and South by Mugford and O'Malley 1990).

The third argument, to be valid in the present context, would involve the return by heavy drug users to normal levels of drug use, and is thus rather more problematic. This is· primarily because current conceptions of addiction do not permit, or enable the definition of, normal drug use. All use of illicit drugs is illegal and therefore 'abnormal', and public perceptions cannot at the present time entertain concepts such as 'normal heroin use' or 'normal cocaine use'. Consequently, the idea of returning to normal levels of drug use from levels that are abnormal cannot be demonstrated, primarily on account of the linguistic and moral contexts surrounding the words 'drugs' and 'normal'. However, progress may be made on this issue if we are prepared to abandon the use of the word 'normal' in favour of a somewhat looser conceptualisation. For example, research from a number of Scottish studies of heroin-and-polydrugs use in the community (O'Doherty and Davies 1988;

Hammersley *et al* 1990) suggests that heroin use typically follows a cyclical pattern. The O'Doherty and Davies study showed a repeated, cyclical pattern of drug use typically of about three-to-four months duration, during which use escalated to a high level. However, use was not maintained at this high level; a period of non-use followed, after which the user was able to get 'cheap highs' once more on fairly modest amounts. The problem for these users was therefore not one of stopping, nor of returning to low levels of use, which many of them were able to do repeatedly; but it must also be said that such levels were characteristically not maintained. Nonetheless, despite this serious flaw in the argument, the idea of compulsive every-day use was not supported, and in the place of a 'compulsion to use' model, a type of cost-benefit analysis seemed to fit the bill better. Users often appeared to control their use spontaneously when the habit reached proportions which lead to too much 'hassle' in terms of economics, time spent finding supplies, risk of detection, value for money, and other practicalities. In an analogous way, the study by Hammersley *et al* revealed that 55% of opioid users used on less than 90% of days; and that roughly 25% of those who had taken opioids in the past had not used during the past year. Once again, however, the available data do not provide unambiguous support for the argument that drug users regularly return to lower and more controlled levels of consumption; and whilst the data from O'Doherty and Davies, and Hammersley *et al*, clearly have something to do with this issue, it is not clear that they address the problem squarely.

Fortunately, there are signs that more direct evidence on this difficult topic may be forthcoming. In the studies by Cohen (*op cit*) and by Ditton (*op cit*), cocaine users were asked to examine a series of graphical representations which depicted their cocaine-use career. These graphical representations, first used by Cohen, are illustrated below. The graphs represent in pictorial form fluctuations in use over time, and drug users are asked to choose the graph which best describes their use career.

In Cohen's Amsterdam study, only 3.1% of respondents chose the classic 'increasing dependency' pattern (graph 2); and the modal choice (39.4%) was graph 4, showing increased use followed by a return to a lower level. According to Cohen, these and other data suggest that typically the cocaine user experiences only 'a relatively short duration of the top period of consumption.' Preliminary data from the Ditton study (*op cit*), for which data are not publicly

I immediately started using large amounts after I first tried cocaine, but gradually decreased since then.

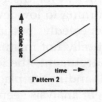

My cocaine use has gradually increased over the years.

I started using cocaine at the same level that I still use, and the amount and frequency haven't changed.

My use increased gradually until it reached a peak, then it decreased.

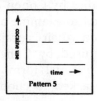

I have started and stopped using cocaine many times.

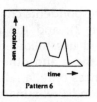

My use pattern has been very varied over the years.

Fig. 3 Patterns of cocaine use (from Cohen P, 1989)

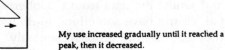

available at the time of writing, show that the same pattern is the modal selection amongst Scottish cocaine users also. Accordingly, whilst one automatically bridles at the concept of a return to normal cocaine use, these data show that users certainly describe returning to more controlled and limited patterns of consumption with some regularity, and of maintaining that reduced level of use over considerable periods of time.

Overall, therefore, there is justification for suggesting that Edwards' line of reasoning should at least be examined to see whether it has applicability where other drugs are concerned. If the case is more difficult to make out, we must acknowledge that there is a shortage of comparable data due to the difficulties of investigating an illegal activity; but in principle there is no reason to argue *a priori* that such a case is necessarily untenable.

Unfortunately, the line of reasoning that led Edwards to suggest that alcoholism was not an 'it' has made less headway in the area of drug 'addiction' than in the specific area of alcohol problems. Whilst specialists with differing areas of expertise will have different detailed perceptions as to the relative importance of different aspects of drug misuse (e.g social, economic, pharmacological, psychological etc) it is nonetheless possible to discern two strands of common meaning which run through the literature, and which appear to be of a categorical nature, whenever the word 'addiction' is used. That is, the use of the word signals that a given group of researchers or treatment specialists, regardless of area of specialisation, have agreed to make certain common judgments about the behaviour in question, which derive from common social perceptions rather than from any particular specialisation or expertise. These judgments are as follows;

i) the word 'addiction' is taken to signify a state. The state is different from the state of being normal though, as in the case of hypnotism, the components of the state remain a mystery. Individuals from different disciplines will, however, have quite different ideas about what the underlying basis of this state is likely to be.

ii) the most salient feature of the supposed state is that it interferes with, or in the extreme case removes, the capacity for voluntary behaviour with respect to a substance or drug. The process which is thought to be responsible for this can range from the 19th century idea of a 'disease of the will' through to more modern conceptions based on biochemistry or pharmacology. Whatever the case, a metaphysical or physical mechanism is proposed which in the extreme case, so it is believed, makes a person unable *not* to take their drug of preference. This inability to make certain types of choice differentiates them from other 'normal' people.

It may be argued that the above characterisation is false, for two reasons. Firstly, some would probably claim that use of the word 'addiction' does not have to imply a state, but may be used to specify a group of people showing a particular behaviour to an extreme degree. In other words, it is merely quantitative. However, whilst this may be true in other instances, it is argued here that psychologically the word is categorical in function, and that sooner or later its categorical nature imposes itself on our thinking. 'Addicted' is the opposite of 'not-addicted' rather than 'less addicted' , and with the sureness of inevitability the categorical nature of the word leads to the search for differences between those who are 'addicted' and those who are 'not addicted'; and subsequently to cures or treatments for those who have 'got it' as opposed to those who 'haven't got it'.

Although it is possible to argue that words like 'addicted' and 'dependent' refer to continuous variables, the postulation of concepts like 'slightly addicted' or 'somewhat dependent' removes from the central concepts most of the denotative or diagnostic value they might otherwise have; and like the oxymoron 'fairly unique', they confuse rather than clarify the issue. The concept of addiction as an 'it' cannot be salvaged by towing it to safety with linguistic qualifiers, like some broken-down vehicle.

The second argument suggests that ultimately there is no difference between 'scientific' explanations (e.g. explanations in terms of the pharmacological impact on neural transmission) and explanations in terms of will-power, decision-making, intentions, and so forth. The latter, it can be argued, are terms of convenience pitched at the level of phenomenology, simply because they refer to events with which no current pharmacology or physiology can deal, but which in principle are explicable ultimately at that level. Consequently, there are not really several competing types of explanation, but only one.

There are a number of rebuttals to this position, both pragmatic and logical. Pragmatically, one can merely say that one will be prepared to accept the usefulness of the pharmacological (or whatever) basis for motives and intentions and so forth, when the day comes that they are understood at that level. However, there is a more fundamental issue to be discussed here, namely that understanding drug action is not the same as understanding the causes of voluntary behaviour. For example, physiological states giving rise to feelings of pain or discomfort are not in themselves sufficient to specify behaviour. People given heroin in hospital seldom become dependent; people will undergo fatigue, stress and even torture rather than divulge a secret; and two 'addicts' can make different decisions about whether to continue use or not. In other words, such decisions derive not just from enteroceptive cues (perception of bodily state) but on the situation in which an individual finds him/herself, as perceived and interpreted by that individual.

Addiction as Disease

The most problematic concept in the addiction area is 'disease'; and despite repeated and consistent assertions in the recent literature that the disease notion has either (a) a highly qualified and constrained application in this area (c.f. the Alcohol Dependence Syndrome), or (b) has no applicability whatsoever (c.f.Heather and Roberston's account of controlled drinking), it remains a notable fact of life that the idea of addiction-as-disease is alive and well amongst many drug and alcohol misusers and their families, and in many treatment agencies. It will not go away for one simple reason. Namely, it is highly functional.

This functionalism will become the main theme of the present book in later chapters, but for the time being we must content ourselves with observing that as a general rule, where a disease interferes with behaviour it replaces something purposive and coordinated with something chaotic (for example, Parkinsons disease, Huntingdon's chorea, peripheral neuritis). Commonsense suggests that the disease definition should indeed normally make reference to something which disrupts or is inimical to integrated and purposive behaviour patterns. It does not make sense as a category description for the replacement of one behaviour with a new, equally integrated, coordinated and purposive pattern. If we postulate a disease which has the direct capacity to force people to steal, to lift up glasses, or to stick needles in their arms when they are actually trying not to, and furthermore to execute long strings of appetitive goal-directed behaviour as precursors to these actions, we have to accept the possibility that any integrated chain of goal directed behaviour in any realm might be nothing more than a disease symptom.

The fact that the short and longer-term disruptions of behaviour which sometimes result from taking drugs can become the occasion for postulating drug taking as a disease manifestation shows a familiar confusion; namely the confusion of intentions with outcomes. For example, during the late 19th and early 20th centuries, missionaries went to Africa where many of them caught malaria and died. The disease was malaria; not the decision to go to Africa. Furthermore, whilst a doctor can in principle treat the malaria, he can only advise people not to go to Africa, on the basis of his own beliefs and opinions about Africa. In a similar way, damage to health caused by drugs does not imply that the decision to take them is pathological, any more than deciding to go to Africa is pathological.

There is little evidence that any disease has the capacity to impose specific integrated behavioural strings in the place of previous ones. However, it may be the case that, in response to the conditions created by a disease, people will voluntarily adopt various strategies to cope with it; and that in a probabilistic sense, some strategies are more useful, and hence more likely, than others. However, these are purposeful and voluntary adaptations to conditions created by the disease, and their inclusion alongside other symptoms creates important dilemmas. Is it reasonable to conceive of the practise of injecting insulin as a symptom of diabetes? If so, where was this symptom before the discovery of insulin therapy? However we resolve this problem, it is clear that, even if we classify such things as symptoms, there is a clear difference in the way the word is being used when (a) we describe something such as high temperature, shortage of breath, or a skin rash, as a symptom, and (b) we talk about going into a pub and buying a pint of beer as a symptom. Whatever we mean by the word 'voluntary' (i.e. whether we take it to imply a metaphysical exercise of the power of 'free will', or a particular mode of cerebellar functioning) it is clear that going into a pub is voluntary in a sense that having a high temperature is not. For these reasons, the inclusion of acts of drug- or alcohol-directed appetitive behaviour as parts of the disease symptomatology, alongside involuntary bodily changes, lumps together two sets of phenomena which require different levels of explanation.

Craving; 'Having to Have', or Just Wanting'?

Within the literature on 'addiction', it is often assumed that voluntary acts are brought into the mainstream of symptomatology by the interaction of two mechanisms. These mechanisms are (a) craving and (b) withdrawal symptoms. These two factors are in some way responsible for the re-classifying of behaviours which are voluntary in normal people as non-voluntary or symptomatic in 'addicts.'

Discussions of the concept of craving are available in Gossop (1990) and in West and Kranzler (1990). In both these pieces of work, the authors accept self-ratings of craving as an indicant of a specific inner (subjective) state, central to which is some sort of compulsive desire which can be accessed through verbal report. It is clear from their discussions, however, that both sets of authors are aware of difficulties with this approach. It appears that there are problems with the concept of craving, especially where this is postulated as an independent entity. In ordinary usage, craving is a response to some basic biological need, giving it an implied compulsive quality, and semantically distinguishing it from a simple want. Thus, lack of food may produce craving for food, and various associated physiological states will give the craving its particular quality. The implication of craving is that the person in question does not simply want, but in some sense has to have, something. The relationship between an emotional state and a bodily state is a thorny one, and goes back at least as far as William James (1884, 1890) who posed some perplexing questions on this issue. Basically James suggested that people do not, for example, run away from a tiger because they feel afraid. Rather, they feel afraid because they perceive the urgency with which they run away from the tiger. Fear, he reasoned, is merely the perception of a bodily state; and in the absence of such a state, the notion of fear *per se* becomes meaningless, a mere idea robbed of its essential ingredients. By analogy, James' idea suggests that people do not seek drugs because they crave, but crave because they seek drugs.

There are a number of criticisms of James' theory, not the least of which is that it ranks alongside other 'mind-as-epiphenomenon' explanations discussed in the introduction. In addition, insufficient types/combinations of discriminable bodily states exist to enable perception of the whole range of felt emotions through this means; for example fear and excitement cannot be readily differentiated in these terms. Nonetheless, it is too easy to couple together the semantic argument that says people use drugs because they feel craving. What is craving for drugs in the absence of perception of bodily state? On what grounds do we postulate an irresistible drive rather than a desire to have? And if craving only makes sense when underlaid by withdrawals, what is the need to postulate it as an independent entity?

In fact, the evidence for the existence of craving is basically that people say they feel it, when asked the appropriate question. Craving cannot be inferred from merely observing behaviour. Thus, in animal experiments, the fact that unfortunate creatures regularly overdosed on some substance suffer from withdrawals and show 'drug-seeking behaviour' is an established fact; but whether the animal craves drugs remains problematic, in the absence of verbal reports from animals. Drug seeking is not in itself evidence of craving if we wish to postulate craving as an independent entity. To have any meaning, the poor creature has to be able to sit and crave quietly to itself, without necessarily going in search of its drug; and even then we cannot assume that it is craving, because there is no independent measure. If we ask a person to say how they feel in such circumstances, however, his/her verbal report will be taken as evidence for an independent craving process. The postulation of craving thus illustrates one more way in which we can be deceived by the preeminence we give to our own verbal behaviour. It illustrates the problem of *reification*, the process whereby a convenient semantic symbol becomes transmuted into an entity which is assumed to have actual existence. In its starkest form, the process involves the psychologist (or whoever) asking someone to provide ratings in terms of some semantic label, on the customary five- or seven-point scale, the labels coming in the first instance from the psychologist. The fact that the subject complies is carelessly taken as proof that the word must refer to something real, an entity; otherwise how could he/she produce systematic ratings? In fact, however, the subject's acquiescence, and subsequent performance, can more parsimoniously be described in terms of the demand characteristics of the interview, and any systematic variation in terms of strategy and response bias, or 'making sense of the task'.

Put simply, craving is an alternative word which we can use to describe an experience of discomfort, and an accompanying desire to curtail or avoid it. If we examine craving from a Kelley-type standpoint, it looks as though a craving explanation is offered in circumstances where i) people consistently choose to reduce their discomfort, and ii) there is a consensus belief about the biological determinants of the discomfort. Thus, whilst drug users 'crave' (have to have) drugs and hungry people 'crave' food, people merely 'want' colour T.V.sets or holidays in Venice. The use of the word 'craving' is an interesting exercise in attribution, and its primary purpose is to convey how we are intended to perceive the addiction process. It refers to the fact that sometimes people feel a strong desire to use, or use more of, their preferred drug, but it gives the impression of an autonomous force whose power cannot be resisted; hence its attraction. In fact, whether people resist the experience depends on whether they have good reasons, or no good reasons, for doing so. People in the dentist's chair have a craving to get up and leave; but by and large they stay put.

Perhaps the last word on the craving issue should be given to a pharmacologist, since it may be assumed in some quarters that the pharmacology of drug action provides a simple and sufficient account of craving as an irresistible force. It is clear however that modern pharmacology takes a more differentiated view. Wise (1990), in an account of 'Reward Pathways and Drug 'Craving' ' (pp 43-45) says the following:

'If there is no depression of reward pathways when chronic use of cocaine or heroin is terminated, what other explanation is there for feelings of drug craving and instances of drug relapse? One possibility is simply that the subject remembers the last reinforcement. . . .'

and later

'Rats clearly remember their last few rewarding brain stimulations, adjusting their speed of running for access to more brain stimulation in proportion to the amount of stimulation received on the last trial. The running speed is the same whether the last trial was five minutes or five days earlier; the rat simply remembers what it has been receiving for lever pressing (Gallistel *et al* 1974). If the rat remembers strong reinforcement, it runs quickly; this has nothing, apparently, to do with the state of its dopamine receptors, since five days should make a difference in any changes in receptor supersensitivity which were caused by the last reinforcement experiment.'

and finally

> 'Craving for cocaine or heroin may, like craving for nicotine in
> a smoker who has been nicotine free for many years, simply be
> triggered by memories of past experience. Like a cat that has
> tasted fish, a human that (sic) has tasted cocaine may be
> unwilling to give up the hope of repeating the experience. If
> this view. . . . . .is correct, then it may be more appropriate to
> look for the biological correlate of craving in the neurobiology
> of memory, and not in the neurobiology of positive reinforce-
> ment.'

Wise (*op cit*) thus implies strongly that craving derives not from
some drug-related change to the reinforcement mechanisms of the
brain which turns a 'want to' into a 'have to'; but more mundanely
from people's simple recollections that some experience was
pleasurable the last time it occurred, coupled to the hope that it
might happen again. In other words, a 'want' deriving from the
normal everyday pharmacology of memory; not a 'have to'
underlaid by some alien drug-induced pharmacology.

Withdrawals

It is necessary to note from the outset that withdrawal symptoms
are real, in the sense that changes to homeostasis brought about by
regular drug use lead to discomfort and temporary illness when the
drug is absent or withdrawn; and that extreme withdrawal
symptoms have been induced in laboratory animals on a number of
occasions (Stewart *et al*, 1984). The most convincing theoretical
argument about possible mechanisms for withdrawals implicates
endogenous opiates, namely the enkephalins, beta-endorphins, and
dynorphins (Bloom 1983). These are opiate-like substances which
occur naturally in the body, and they have the function of
inhibiting neurotransmitters and so producing analgesia. Taking
opiate drugs over a prolonged period makes the role of the
endogenous opiates redundant in some sense, and their production
is therefore reduced as part of a homeostatic feedback mechanism.
When the opiate drug is withdrawn the body is left without its
natural analgesic defences against over-activity in the excitatory
systems (Johnston 1990).

However, whilst withdrawals are real enough and convincing

pharmacological models exist to explain their existence, it is also the case that the precise nature and extent of the symptoms, particularly the behavioural manifestations, are not uniquely specified by the drug and its pharmacological effects. The form taken by withdrawals, their severity, and the significance attached to them by the sufferer, depend on a variety of situational and cognitive factors in addition to straightforward pharmacological effects. This has been demonstrated with animals as well as observed with people. For example, rats orally addicted to morphine show physiological and behavioural signs of withdrawal when in their customary cage (i.e.the cage where the addiction process took place); but show more exploratory behaviour and less external signs of withdrawal when in a new and different cage. More importantly, the animals show greater avidity for morphine solution during the 're-addiction' phase when in the cage where the original addiction has been acquired (Thompson and Ostlund, 1965) than in the changed environment.

An even more striking demonstration of the way in which withdrawals depend on contextual factors, and thus cannot be conceptualised as some sort of powerhouse or driving force for future drug use, was provided by MacRae and Seigal (unpublished; cited in Balfour 1990, p.81) in an experiment with 'yoked' rats. Rats worked in trios, each member being in a different cage. One rat could self-administer morphine through a cannula, by means of a lever press. The second animal passively received the same dose at the same times as the first animal by means of a yoked or 'slave' syringe pump, but could not actively self-administer. A third control animal passively received Ringer solution, also in a yoked manner. The experiment ran for six days, but on the seventh day no drugs were available to any animal. On the seventh day there was a clear and substantial difference between the animals in terms of withdrawal distress, with the rat who actively self-administered showing by far the most severe symptoms. The authors conclude:

'It would appear that interoceptive signals of a drug, incidental to voluntary self-administration, can importantly influence the magnitude of withdrawal symptoms.' (The reader's attention is specifically drawn to the use of the word 'voluntary', which is essential to making phenomenological sense of this study, despite its underlying determinist philosophy.)

At the human level it can be observed that the florid withdrawal symptoms portrayed in films like 'The French Connection' are by no means typical, and that prisoners on remand who endure forced withdrawals from heroin often seem to suffer from something more like an attack of influenza, rather than screaming and clawing at the walls. Finally, just to confuse the issue, many of us will have seen spoiled children who can writhe about on the floor and make themselves sick if mummy refuses to give them another Easter Egg.

This variability creates the final dilemma. If, as seems to be the case, there is variability in severity of withdrawals as a function of time, place, expectation or whatever, then it becomes increasingly difficult to conceptualise withdrawals as the basic powerhouse or engine-room for 'addictive' behaviour. Furthermore, since we have argued that 'craving' lacks its essential property of compulsion, so 'addiction' becomes less monolithic and more amenable to explanation in human terms.

Cures for Taking Drugs

Returning to our main theme, it is suggested that the concept of 'addiction' might conceivably have some value if it gave emphasis to the normal and nonpathological decisions people make about drugs; but in fact it is usually employed to encapsulate certain assumptions about what drugs do to people, thereby implying a process from which the powers, wishes and intentions of the drug user are specifically excluded. The idea that the pharmacology of drugs makes people into addicts against their 'will' has to be contrasted with the idea that people make addicts of themselves because they choose to do so. The latter is a challenging suggestion which deserves serious consideration, and it certainly makes sense of the fact that treatment for addictions frequently seems to have more in common with procedures for attitude change, than with medical intervention.

From such a standpoint, the term 'addiction' appears to refer not so much to some medical condition as to certain disapproved-of ways of thinking and deciding, certain acts of choice which are not qualitatively or quantitatively different from thinking, deciding and choosing in any other area of human life, but which happen to involve drugs. Because of the pharmacological action of drugs, the consequences can be disastrous to health, family and all aspects of living, but such consequences do not in themselves warrant the postulation of a special state which compels their use. Furthermore, there is no cure for drug taking because there is fundamentally nothing to be cured; no more in fact than there is a cure for rock climbing, football, or playing the violin. But if there are reasons for supposing that in a given case the rock climbing, football, or violin-playing are resulting in social and economic problems for the individual and for others, one might try to persuade him/her to reappraise the basis on which they make their decisions.

Because the basic decision to take drugs, notwithstanding the consequences of excessive use, is fundamentally non-pathological, much of the research into 'addictions' which seeks a better understanding of why people drink too much, smoke too much, or take drugs, is in reality a search for why people decide to do, commit themselves to, or dedicate themselves to, anything. Insofar as the search is for an understanding of the whole of human 'choice' behaviour, one can expect that no sudden breakthrough will occur; the search can go on more or less indefinitely. Furthermore, from some perspectives the problem appears to confound alternative metaphysical (i.e. free will) and materialist (i.e. determinist) propositions which can never be explained under a common rubric. In other words, the underlying philosophy is flawed. Within such a framework, theoretical progress becomes more a matter of good luck than of good management; and practical progress hinges on reactive and short-term expediencies, rather than presenting any clear or realistic view of how drug use fits into society in the longer term.

In Conclusion

Certain central features of the received wisdom about drug addicts and addiction have to be challenged. The idea that addiction is a state in which the driving force for autonomous action becomes lost to the individual, and is taken over by craving, an irresistible psychological force fuelled by inevitable and excruciating withdrawal symptoms, is untenable since these concepts do not in fact possess the monolithic properties that they would require in order to assume the roles assigned to them. In their place, we require a conception of drug use which restores the user to centre stage, and within which his/her motives and intentions within particular contexts become the focus for attention and future theoretical development.

5

Pharmacology and Compulsion

Degree of compulsion-to-use, or 'addictiveness', has long been seen as varying between different substances. There is irrefutable evidence of differences in pharmacological action between individual drugs, as well as at the broader level of categorisations such as CNS stimulants and depressants. A number of texts are available which provide accounts of the pharmacological action of different psychotropic substances, and no purpose is served here in simply relaying information which is readily available elsewhere. However, given the current concern about cocaine and its derivative, crack, it seems appropriate to use this as an example in the context of the current discussion, with the proviso that the basis of the argument is the same for other drugs also.

It is widely held that crack cocaine has uniquely addictive properties, and this idea is reiterated not only in the popular press, but also in the more straight-laced media. For example, the 'Observer' newspaper (Browne, 1988) carried a full-page feature on crack in which it was reported that according to unidentified 'experts', three out of four first-time users became 'instantly addicted'. From this standpoint, the article goes on to attribute a variety of other behaviours, which clearly have an economic basis, to the action of the drug itself. For example:

> 'Because of its volatile effect on the user and its addictive qualities, crack leads to a significant increase in violence, muggings, burglaries, theft and other crimes.'

In fact, most theft of whatever type stems from the desire of

56

people wanting something, but not having the economic resources to realise their ambition. This is true of cocaine, but it also true of colour-television sets, motor-yachts, and bars of chocolate. The fact that poor people who want drugs steal in order to get them hardly amounts to a major insight into the motivators of theft.

However, more problematic is the assertion that cocaine has the capacity to be instantly addictive. The available evidence reveals that cocaine and crack have rapid, but short-lived, pharmacological effects of a fairly dramatic nature, these varying (as with all drugs) as a function of the purity of the drug and the mode of administration. Other things being equal, injection produces the most rapid hit, but with cocaine the effect lasts for about 20 minutes via this route, whereas the effect from snorting lasts longer but is said to be less intense and 'smoother'. Crack is relatively new, and consists of cocaine with the alkaloid component driven off by various simple means, such as heating the drug in a microwave oven together with baking powder. Because of its recency, the precise pharmacology of crack is less well documented, but verbal reports suggest the hit is very rapid due to increased volatility, almost analogous to injection with the parent substance, cocaine.

Cocaine and crack produce increases in certain neurotransmitters in parts of the brain, neurotransmitters being chemical 'messengers' that assist in the transmission of impulses between nerve cells. Cocaine causes increases in the levels of monoamines, notably dopamine, a chemical transmitter that is to varying degrees lacking in sufferers from Parkinson's disease but which is often present to excess in schizophrenics, where its causal influence is a matter for some debate. However, cocaine is a monoamine oxidase inhibitor (MAOI), which means to say that it achieves its effect of increasing monoamine levels NOT by stimulating their production but by inhibiting their re-uptake by those cells that normally carry out this function. In other words, it inhibits reabsorption, rather than stimulating production. The detailed pharmacology has been revealed in recent studies by Bozarth (1990) and by White (1990) in studies of rats.

Such pharmacological studies almost certainly reveal the mechanism underlying cocaine's pleasurable effects, and consequently why it is used for recreational purposes. They also enable comparisons with other drugs to be made, and provide support for statements about the relative intensity and differing quality of different-drug experiences. Clark (1990) for example, showed that even rats could discriminate between the subjective effects of different drugs, using an operant (lever-pressing) paradigm.

From this point, however, the mythology of addiction takes on a curious turn. The next inference stems from the preference for a particular form of explanation rather than from the inductive logic of science, and asserts that the person 'has to have' the drug, and 'has no choice' but to use it. There is, of course, nothing in the pharmacology itself that justifies such an inference, which signals a change in preferred philosophy rather than a change in fact. The problem of whether any behaviour is mechanistic or volitional hinges around definitions and beliefs. At the end of the day, any mechanistic (logical positivistic) interpretation requires a phar-macological/physiological basis for *all* action, so the specification of cocaine use as being non-volitional because it has a demonstrable pharmacology fails to distinguish it from any other behaviour and any other pharmacology. Drug taking cannot be seen as *more determined* since there is no behaviour which is *less determined*, unless the determinist is, paradoxically, prepared to allow meta-physics to enter the equation.

It is interesting to ask why it is that on the basis of evidence which is inappropriate to the purpose (namely the discovery that cocaine has, unsurprisingly, a knowable pharmacology), the non-logical conclusion is derived that 'therefore' cocaine-related be-haviour is quite different in fundamental principle from 'ordinary' behaviour with respect to philosophical imponderables like 'free will' and 'volition'. The reasons why this happens will be discussed in detail in a later chapter.

However, the suggestion that drug-related behaviour is in some sense automatic is supported by another body of evidence which is less easily dismissed. A number of workers have performed variants of an experiment in which some small animal, normally a rat, has a cannula inserted into its brain through which tiny amounts of drug can be administered to selected sites. In a paper by Bozarth (*op cit*) originally entitled 'The Pre-eminence of Animal Studies in Comparative Substance Use', but subsequently pub-lished under a more modest heading (1990) a number of studies are described in which rats, surgically prepared as described above, are placed in a Skinner-type box. The lever-pressing response delivers measured amounts of drug to locations in the rat's brain. In these circumstances, the rat shows a pattern of lever pressing which, from the point of view of the observer, appears to be to be compulsive and automatic (see chapter 3). The rat presses the lever to obtain drug in preference to all other behaviours including eating and if left to its own devices the rat will eventually starve.

The question that now arises is the extent to which this situation serves as a model for the behaviour of human beings, seeking out their drug of choice despite the possible negative consequences of this behavioural focus. The standard rebuttal to claims that animal studies can actually shed light on human action is usually some type of comparative argument, the essential gist of which is that animals are basically deficient in ways that people believe are important; and consequently one cannot make inferences from one to the other willy-nilly. However, whatever the virtues of this argument, the fact that it can be trotted out whenever necessary as a way of defending against anyone who would argue for phylogenetic continuity in behaviour, makes it somewhat unsatisfactory. In the present circumstances, a more satisfactory argument concerns the demand characteristics of the experimental situation.

Rather than claiming that humans are not like rats, it seems equally reasonable to suggest that people in the same situation as the rat would behave in very much the same way. Studies of deprivation and confinement do indeed reveal fundamental changes to what would be described as normal human behaviour, among which is the increased significance that becomes attached to events that would normally be regarded as trivial (Watson 1978). Furthermore, the real analogy is not from the rat in the Skinner box to the drug user in the street; but from the drug user in the street to the rat in his/her accustomed environment. It is almost certain that given a normal environment in which to explore and wander, and a means of ingesting the drug which makes sense to the rat, the hapless creature will show more variety of behaviour than is revealed in the Skinner box. A telling experiment was performed by Johnson and Johnson (1972) with Siamese fighting fish. The fish, placed in a type of aquatic Skinner box, had been previously shown to display 'automatic' aggression whenever a suitable sign-stimulus (e.g. another fish) was introduced. The fish appeared to seek out such aggressive encounters, to find them highly rewarding, and to do little else besides. However, in truth there was little else to do. When Johnson and Johnson introduced a variety of stimuli into the environment, the fish worked harder to obtain sight of these novelties. What looked like an automatic and inevitable drive towards aggression turned into something more like curiosity and exploration when a more varied set of alternatives was offered.

The crucial study in the present context would thus involve observing whether rats, taught to use some drug, would seek out that drug to the exclusion of all else when offered an environment comparable in variety and richness to that normally available to rats. Though the precise study has not been carried out, logic suggests that the answer would almost certainly be 'No'. Consequently, with respect to the reasons why people and animals use drugs, the animal studies show little except that ethologically senseless environments produce ethologically ridiculous behaviours.

However, although no study has been performed which compares rats in boxes to rats in a natural environment, and the effect of this manipulation upon drug self-administration through an ethologically sensible route, two studies have been performed which come quite close to this ideal. In a study by Alexander, Coambs and Hadaway (1978), rats living in isolation in standard laboratory cages were compared to rats living socially in a large open box. The rats were exposed to a series of three-day reinforcement cycles previously shown by Nichols *et al* to increase oral self-administration (drinking) of morphine solution. These cycles are referred to as periods of 'forced consumption'. Subsequently, when 'choice days' were introduced during which the rats could choose either morphine solution or water, the isolated/caged rats drank more morphine than the social rats. The authors write:

> 'A possible explanation is that. . . ..for the isolated rats the reinforcement value of morphine ingestion was enhanced by relief of the discomfort of spatial confinement, social isolation and stimulus deprivation. Similarly, in the social group, the reinforcement value of morphine may have been diminished by it's interference with the rat's natural activity patterns.'

And later:

> 'A housing-condition effect, if substantiated, needs to be accounted for by existing theories of addiction. Conditioning theories of opiate addiction generally state that self-administration of opiates is reinforced by relief of withdrawal symptoms. In this study, the effectiveness of training procedures specifically based on this principle. . . .appeared to be environment specific. Not only did the social group ingest less morphine than the isolated group during the choice days of the Nichols Cycle Period, but they *decreased* their consumption while the

isolated rats *increased* theirs. A neurochemical change theory would also need to account for a housing conditions effect.'

In a further study, Alexander *et al* (1981) took things a step further by examining the effect of early, as opposed to later, colony housing on oral ingestion of morphine by rats. Rats housed socially at the time of testing drank less of a morphine-hydrochloride (MHCl) solution than did isolated rats, but drank no less of control solutions. Colony-dwelling rats who had been previously isolated drank more MHCl solution than did rats reared in a social setting since weaning, but only at the lower MHCl concentrations. Analysis of variance of the data showed only a significant main effect for conditions of housing at the time of testing; the effects of early environment were insignificant, though there was a marginally (0.06) significant interaction. The authors suggest that colony rats avoided opiates because opiate consumption interfered with the performance of complex species-specific social behaviours that had no relevance when the rat was artificially isolated.

Self-Reports from Humans

Despite the above arguments, it is regularly observed by clinicians that clients with drug problems report feelings of loss-of-control and lack of volition. These statements are frequently expressed in such earnest and self-deprecatory terms that to suggest clients are liars, or simply deluded, hardly seems to do justice to the horror of the situation. It is statements such as these that tend to become enshrined in the work on drug action; and in consequence the pharmacological quest becomes a search for 'scientific proof' to back up the verbal reports. However, there is a basic misconception about the nature of statements from drug users who so regularly assert that they 'cannot stop'. The statements themselves are not 'scientific' in the first place, but functional. The earnestness with which the statements are made attest to their functional necessity, rather than their literal truth.

Bem (1968; 1972) suggested that people make inferences about others on the basis of observing what they do. Thus, our beliefs and knowledge of others are derived from observations, on the basis of which we make inferences. However, Bem went on to say that we make inferences about our own behaviour in exactly the same way.

When a person reports not being able to control their drug use, we are in error if we assume they are revealing first-hand (proximate) knowledge about the fundamental principles underlying their behaviour. Rather, such reports are socially-functional inferences deriving from self observation.

If we observe that, with great regularity, we over-indulge in some activity to the detriment of health, family, friends and economic functioning, we require a linguistic formula that enables us to explain these circumstances in an acceptable fashion. *The statement that 'I cannot stop' is not a statement of fact, but an inference based on the self-observation that I reliably fail to do so.*

The statement 'I cannot stop' is thus primarily a metaphor; and no other linguistic device adequately captures the moral and behavioural dilemma in which the 'addict' finds him/herself.

6

The Problem of 'Addictive Substances'

In terms of *locus*, the addiction concept has a foot in two camps. That is to say, it can be used to describe something which arises due to the 'addictive' properties of particular substances; but we can also use the word to refer to a latent property of people who become 'addicts'. In fact, this is entirely sensible so long as drug problems are conceptualised as resulting from the interaction of people with substances, both of which have their own individual characteristics. Problems arise however if we imagine that either, alone, is sufficient to create 'addiction' in the absence of the other; that is, if we visualise addiction as a straightforward consequence of using some substance, or as an inherent and inevitable property of particular kinds of people. In Chapter 4 we examined the ways in which Edwards was drawn to conclude that no special group of people could be identified who inevitably became 'alcoholic'; and in a similar way the case was put forward that no special group of 'drug addicts', differing in some respect from the rest of the population, could be identified either. However, there are two components in the equation, namely people and substances, and just as we may carelessly from time to time imply that characteristics of people are a sole and sufficient condition for the development of addictions, so we also sometimes imply that a substance is all that is required.

Different illicit substances are regularly described as differentially addictive, particularly (but not exclusively) in popular media accounts; thereby giving rise to the implication that drugs are underlaid by some sort of continuum in terms of a latent propensity

63

to cause addiction, though people disagree about its precise nature. Thus, in most people's minds a principal feature of heroin is its inherent 'capacity to addict,' and this idea is reinforced in the popular press by reports of celebrated addicts from the world of music and entertainment, who readily provide heroin testimonials centring around the legend 'I tried it once, and I was hooked', or some similar explanation for their behaviour. On the other hand, the drug ecstasy (an amphetamine-type drug) is regularly asserted to be non-addictive, as at various times have all the amphetamine-type drugs, and cocaine. In more recent times, however, the picture has changed and the addictive properties of cocaine and its derivative, crack, are now graphically described in the press, accompanied by fears of an anticipated crack epidemic.

It remains only to say that beliefs about which drugs are highly addictive and which are not are as variable and fashion-prone as the latest clothes or popular-music charts. Cannabis, described by a U.S. senator as the most evil and corrupting substance known to mankind during the 1930's, is now seen as 'soft', as relatively harmless, and in some circles as scarcely meriting its legal classification. By contrast, cocaine, seen in the 1950's as safe and non-dependency forming, is now viewed as highly dangerous, with addictive properties so compelling that a majority of people who try the drug are believed to become addicted immediately.

In fact, there is no substance or activity that cannot become the focus for an obsessive or 'addicted' type of behaviour from someone; and conversely there is no drug that has the capacity to elicit such behaviour from anyone. Similarly, all the evidence suggests that whilst there is some genetic basis for addiction, it has very little predictive or explanatory power viewed in isolation from other factors. Anyone can become 'an addict'; and conversely no-one is doomed to be an addict by their inheritance.

These two competing but psychologically complementary views of addiction, as either a property of people or substances, are extremely useful, because we can hop between the two types of explanation according to circumstance. When talking about people, we can distance ourselves from those who 'suffer from addiction'; and when talking about our own alcohol or cigarette use, we can distance these drugs from substances that are 'more addictive'. This choice of possible explanations is one of the hallmarks of functional attribution, since we can use one or the other according to which side of an argument we wish to support.

Given that people and drugs can both have, apparently, characteristics which are to a greater or lesser extent 'addictive', the choice of either one of these domains as the locus of explanation for the plight of any individual is a matter of preferred explanation. A given person in a given drug-related situation can be 'explained' because he/she has certain addictive propensities, or because he/she fell prey to certain addictive substances. Unfortunately, the relationship between characteristics of people on the one hand, and of different substances on the other, and the way in which they actually interact to produce specified outcomes in particular social and economic circumstances, is an issue of such subtlety that it has never been successfully researched. Nonetheless, we may shed some light on the issue by examining the grey no-man's land where one of the two crucial variables (i.e. addiction as a property of people; addiction as a property of substances) is missing. This is the area where addiction occurs in the absence of an externally administered drug, gambling being the classic example. By examining this phenomenon we may come to a better understanding of the way in which a substance itself contributes to the situation, and whether or not such an external agent is necessary if a behaviour is to have those features that we describe as 'addicted'. First, however, we must touch on the difficult issue of 'real' and 'bogus' addicts which is sometimes raised when we start to discuss putative addictions which have no basis in an external pharmacology.

The Issue of 'Real' and 'Bogus' Addicts

Certain radical perspectives in addiction research in the U.K. emerged in the area of alcohol problems, and the two texts by Heather and Robertson which were mentioned in a previous chapter provided a stimulus for new thinking on the topic, as well as raising hackles in various quarters. It will be recalled that the topic which caused the most furore was the issue of controlled drinking, first raised by D.L.Davies in the pages of the *Quarterly Journal of Studies on Alcohol* (1962), and explored further in a number of other papers (1969; 1969 *et al*).

So-called controlled drinking, it is claimed, is the capacity of 'alcoholics' to return to normal controlled patterns of consumption. From certain viewpoints, the suggestion that controlled drinking is not merely possible but that it exists and is not so difficult to find, strikes at the heart of certain customary ways of viewing alcohol addiction. At the theoretical level, it threatens the central role of *reinstatement of symptoms*, an important component of the disease model which states that a recovering alcoholic will rapidly return to an alcoholic drinking pattern unless abstinence is maintained. At an everyday level it causes consternation amongst those who support an Alcoholics Anonymous or similar '12-step' type of philosophy, and who have an ideological commitment to abstinence as the only route to sobriety.

In the face of D.L.Davies' claims, attempts were made in some quarters to defend the disease model of alcoholism with a somewhat unsatisfactory piece of circular logic. *Any alcoholic who successfully returned to controlled drinking was never an alcoholic in the first place.*

It is not necessary to comment in detail upon the 'Heads I win; tails you lose' nature of arguments of this type. However, an interesting paradox is created in the case of a person with severe alcohol problems, who at a later stage in his/her career returns to controlled drinking. Whilst experiencing drinking problems, this person has probably had no difficulty in winning the accolade 'alcoholic'. Indeed, everyone has probably been trying to persuade him/her to accept this view; perhaps even characterising any arguments to the contrary as 'alcoholic denial'. However, if this person later succeeds in returning to a more controlled pattern of consumption, he/she has to accept that the earlier conceptual framework was wrong. So if the person was not really an 'alcoholic', what was happening?

Apparently, the disease of alcoholism is of such a problematic nature that a definitive diagnosis can only be made in circumstances where the patient recovers; in which case we may say with certainty, according to the circular logic of the argument, that he/she never had 'it'. Furthermore, it begins to look as though those who 'recover' and who were thus never real alcoholics, were therefore doing 'it' on purpose; and they did not 'recover' in any meaningful sense of the word. They merely decided to stop.

Unfortunately this implies that the known population of 'alcoholics' at any one time consists of two indistinguishable subgroups, 'real alcoholics' who are driven to drink by forces beyond their capacity to control and 'bogus alcoholics' who might decide to stop misusing alcohol at any moment. How are we to tell them apart? The problem is in fact not resolvable without recourse to different-level constructs or definitions, but the issue about 'real' and 'bogus' alcoholics is raised here because a similar type of argument sometimes emerges in the discussion about whether excessive (or so-called compulsive) gamblers are 'real' addicts or not.

The absence of an 'addictive substance' is sometimes the only cue for the argument that they cannot really be addicts because there is no substance involved for them to be addicted to; and consequently gamblers are not true addicts but in some sense 'do it on purpose.' The problem of the locus of addiction is nicely illustrated here, since in this instance one viewpoint sees addiction to gambling as an internal property of people, so no external drug is required; whereas the other suggests that addiction requires an addictive drug, or otherwise there is nothing to 'cause addiction'.

The Compulsive Gambler

The most striking feature of the literature on gambling is the similarity between the language employed and the language of the other addictions. The same issues arise with regularity and are addressed in familiar terms. A readable text on this issue has been provided by Dickerson in the book *Compulsive Gamblers* (1984). Dickerson points to a number of authors who have described the behaviours associated with 'problem gambling' variously as compulsive, addicted and pathological; the latter two of which clearly imply something categorical and specifically outwith the range of the normal. One strand of the book then points out the difficulties of demonstrating how these 'special' people differ from other 'normal' regular and frequent gamblers.

It appears that 'compulsive' gamblers tend to be older than regular high-frequency gamblers; a finding which emerged from a study comparing Gamblers Anonymous members who had a history of off course betting with a group of similar betters who were not GA members. Only a small proportion of women are regular off-course betters (about 2%), and in the U.K. this is reflected in the fact that only about 2% of GA members are women. After these suggestions that there may be age and sex differences, however, it becomes increasingly difficult to find specific characteristics of 'addicted' as opposed to high-frequency gamblers.

Dickerson reviews evidence for and against the idea that various psychological and behavioural characteristics may differentiate high-frequency gamblers from those who are 'compulsive', and the outcome is highly reminiscent of similar lines of research in the field of alcohol and drug problems.

The more or less fruitless search for 'the alcoholic personality' and the 'addictive personality' seem to parallel similar efforts to uncover the defining personality characteristics of compulsive gamblers; and the outcome is hardly any more reassuring. Dickerson cites work from a number of authors who have shown differences between compulsive gamblers and test norms for a number of dimensions, including locus of control, extroversion, neuroticism, social and emotional adjustment, impulsivity, and intelligence. However, with two exceptions, the studies cited compare scores with test norms obtained in the process of test standardisation rather than with matched control groups, a situation that finds many parallels in the addiction field. Of the two better studies, (Wong 1980; Malkin 1981) one finds elevated locus-of-control scores whilst the other does not. In a similar way, there are a number of studies of smokers and drinkers which have shown differences between users and 'normal' subjects in terms of cognitive style and locus of control, and others which have found no such differences. For example, Lilienfeld (1959), Straits and Sechrest (1963) and James, Woodruff and Werner (1965) found smokers to be more external than non-smokers; whilst Lichtenstein and Keutzer (1967) and Christiano (1970) found no differences. Similarly, Goss and Morosko (1970) and Gozali (1971) found 'alcoholics' to be more internal than population norms, whilst Nadrith (1975) found them to be more external. In all these cases, absence of a strong theory, and lack of comparability between the studies, makes the findings uninterpretable. Furthermore, we have argued in an earlier chapter that the theoretical basis for the expectation that addicts might differ from non-addicts in terms of locus of control or internality/externality is fundamentally flawed from the outset at a theoretical level.

Reviewing his gambling evidence, Dickerson concludes, '..there are insurmountable problems of interpretation' (page 41), and later, 'In the absence of any normative data for gamblers on intelligence or personality measures, it is impossible to evaluate scores from groups of compulsive gamblers selected on the basis of their attendance for treatment.' These conclusions would apply to much of the evidence from smoking and drinking studies also.

Preferred form of gambling is another topic of interest. The compulsive gambler, by repute, is hooked on the act of gambling and will bet on anything given the opportunity to do so. An interesting aspect of different forms of gambling is the idea that compulsive gamblers may choose outlets which are more dangerous and more compulsive; an argument which parallels the idea of highly-addictive substances. On the one hand, raffle tickets and football pools are considered relatively safe forms of betting, and there are few, if any, reports in the literature of people seeking help for problems arising from these. On the other hand, forms which involve rapid and continuing sequences of betting, as in betting on horse or dog races, seem more dangerous or more 'addictive'. The literature on gambling has addressed this problem, and a number of workers have related the apparently 'addictive' nature of off-course betting,(i.e. in the betting shop) to such factors as the pacing of the betting sequence by the in-shop T.V. coverage, and the cyclical sequence of excitement and denouement. Last-minute betting and associated high arousal levels seem to be important features (e.g. Brown R.I.F., 1988; Dickerson, Hinchy and Fabre, 1987).

It appears that compulsive gamblers indulge most often in forms having these 'addictive' characteristics. However, it is also certainly the case that the larger proportion of people indulging in these more addictive forms do not seek treatment, nor do they see themselves as 'compulsive gamblers' or 'addicted'. In a similar way, whilst the law and the media see heroin users as 'addicts', it is not difficult to find regular users who do not see themselves in these terms, who manage to maintain some sort of normal family life and hold down a job (see for example Stimson and Oppenheimer, 1982 *op cit*). On this issue, Dickerson concludes that in fact compulsive gamblers and high-frequency gamblers cannot be differentiated in terms of number or type of betting outlets. He writes, 'Compulsive gamblers and high-frequency gamblers seem to demonstrate similar patterns of betting behaviour,' and notes simply that these might differ from the behaviours of average or less frequent gamblers. As with the search for the personality dimensions which differentiate heavy regular drinkers from 'alcoholics', one has to conclude at the end of the day that the search for those characteristics which differentiate compulsive from normal heavy gamblers has failed.

There is a detectable imbalance between out-moded and lay theories of gambling as residing in essentially mechanistic and pathological ideas of compulsion, and more recent cognitive formulations based on decision making, subjectively rational choice, reversal theory and hedonism, illusion of control, attributional style, and so forth. (e.g. Langer 1975; Frank and Smith; Rosecrance 1986; Gilovitch 1983; Brown 1988 *op cit*; Anderson and Brown 1987). All of these latter suggestions offer distinct advantages over theories based on pathology. However, the general position adopted here is perhaps most succinctly expressed by David Oldman in his paper Compulsive Gamblers (Oldman 1978). Amongst a number of important insights, Oldman includes the following:

> 'Accounts of gambling which make reference to more or less precisely articulated theories of compulsion are prevalent as 'lay' accounts amongst those who have little experience of gambling and particularly amongst the predominantly protestant crusades against gambling. 'Expert' accounts of compulsion appear only in the therapeutic literature, particularly in psychoanalysis, using as source material the self reports of gamblers who are patients. It is probable. . . ..that theories of compulsion figure prominently in the legal defence of persons on trial for embezzlement and theft when the money has been used to finance gambling.'

Oldman continues, 'Where an immoral activity is the product of defect rather than deviance, one stands in no danger of posing a counter-ideology . . . .'. Finally, Oldman makes the crucial point that habitual gamblers may well feel that they do not have an acceptable 'vocabulary of motive' to justify their abandonment of domestic and economic responsibilities; and that the shift from talking in terms of motive to talking in terms of compulsion occurs 'only when financial crisis hits'.

This last point indicates that the functional nature of explanation, and in particular the value of the compulsion argument, is well known to some workers in the area of gambling. Oldman's conclusion is in principle the same as some of the conclusions arising from our own research studies, which will be discussed in detail in later chapters. For example, 'The idea that an 'addict' is nothing more or less than a person who has become accustomed to explaining that he/she is one, deserves serious contemplation.' (Coggans and Davies 1988); and also,'. . . the problem of drug misuse is a problem of being unable to resist temptation and this has a moral rather than a medical significance; . . . an addict is someone who continues to take heroin but believes that he or she should stop taking heroin.' (Hammersley, Morrison, Davies and Forsyth, 1987). A very similar type of message also emerges from Orford's (1984) text 'Excessive Appetites', and it is apposite to conclude this section with two short quotes from that author (pp217).

> 'It is not just that 'addiction' is not apparent until a person wishes to give up drug use or until other people put pressure upon him or her to do so, but rather that the very notion of drug 'dependence' has no meaning until such circumstances pertain'

and also

> '. . . .drug dependence can only be seen to exist to the degree that pressure is put upon the individual, or some incentive offered him, to reduce his drug taking. . . .and the argument applies in my view with equal force to non-drug forms of strong appetite such as excessive heterosexuality, excessive gambling, and over-eating.'

Alcoholics Anonymous and Gamblers Anonymous

The suggestion that compulsive gamblers cannot be differentiated from heavy regular gamblers, and the implication derived therefrom that the distinction might not exist, is resisted by problem-gamblers (i.e. gamblers experiencing problems) for the same reasons that the preservation of a distinction between heavy drinking and alcoholism is important to drinkers. It forms the corner-stone of a functional disease model of addiction which is applied both to gamblers and drinkers as appropriate, and defines the behaviours in question in terms of a 'state' which has to be 'treated'; that is, as pathological. Like the notion of addiction as applied to alcohol (and other drugs) the notion of addiction to gambling removes the personal responsibility of the heavy gambler for his/her single-minded pursuit of gambling activity.

It is apparent that in circumstances where problems arise the perception of gambling and drinking as disease manifestations can become a central feature of gamblers' and drinkers' self perceptions. However, bearing in mind that the basis for the postulation of alcoholism as disease resides in an inborn predisposition or 'allergy' with respect to a specific 'addictive' substance, whereas no such substance-specific vulnerability underlies gambling, it is indeed remarkable that similar explanations for the two phenomena can be produced with so few apparent logical difficulties. On this particular point, it is interesting to note that the ideological underpinnings of Alcoholics Anonymous and Gamblers Anonymous are almost interchangeable in some respects.

'What is the first thing a compulsive gambler ought to do in order to stop gambling? He must accept the fact that he is in the grip of a progressive illness. . . .' The above extract is taken from a Gamblers Anonymous pamphlet cited by Dickerson (*op cit*). The pamphlet continues with the 'one drink, one drunk' argument, now placed in a new setting: 'The first small bet to a gambler is like the first small drink to an alcoholic.' Furthermore, the recommended regime for both conditions is strikingly similar, and has a standard religious basis which, in attributional terms, involves transference of individual will to a deity or some higher power. 'We came to believe that a power greater than ourselves could restore us to sanity' is the Second Step of AA philosophy, and compares readily with the recovery programme for gamblers prescribed by Gamblers Anonymous; 'Most of us feel that a belief in a Power greater than ourselves is necessary in order to sustain a desire to refrain from gambling.'

There are numerous other examples of the ways in which AA and GA philosophy and teaching overlap, and these similarities have clearly struck other authors too. Indeed, Stewart and Brown (1988) have even suggested, since AA keeps no records of its clients success or failure as a matter of principle, that their own results from Gamblers Anonymous 'give a more accurate picture of a self-help group almost identical to AA than has hitherto been possible. It is likely, then, that the present findings represent a more reliable estimate of the efficacy of AA than has hitherto been possible.'

The Role of Internally-Produced States

Normally, addiction to gambling is brought into line with addiction to substances by reference to people's capacity to produce their own internal addictive substances, or their own internal addictive states. For example, Dickerson, Hinchy and Fabre (1987 *op cit*) write,

'. . . .even in the absence of a psychoactive agent, many repetitions of extreme physiological states of arousal may be sufficient to generate an addictive pattern of behaviour.' Furthermore, the fact that people can produce their own internal drugs (endorphines) can be used to argue that therefore gambling is a substance-based addiction just like addiction to drugs.

However, this argument for a unified substance-based theory of addiction has a major shortcoming. The idea that people can generate their own internal addictive pharmacology can be applied to all sorts of behaviours other than gambling and drug-taking, including such valued activities as playing the violin, walking to the North Pole, or becoming a Member of Parliament; things which in themselves are not regarded as pathological. Consequently, if we adopt this line of argument, any type of commitment or dedication stands in danger of becoming an 'addiction', especially if the person feels good as a consequence.

The fact that two such different phenomena as problem drinking and problem gambling, one underlaid by a pharmacologically active substance, and one not so underlaid, (except insofar as people can and do produce their own endorphines and high-arousal states in connection with all sorts of activities *most of which are not seen as addictions*) come to be viewed in the same terms leads one to postulate that the real reason for the common explanation derives not from commonality of causality or process, but from the *common functions served by that type of explanation.*

Pursuing this line of thinking further, we may conclude this chapter by asking the question whether, independent of the evidence for the truth or falsity of the 'disease of addiction', there are any other instances in which explanation in terms of disease is applied to behaviours which require explanation in non-voluntary terms because explanation in terms of personal responsibility might imply 'bad'? To the extent that such explanations exist, it could then be shown that the explanation of drug use in terms of addiction is not unique in being primarily socially functional, rather than scientifically veridical.

7

Disease as the Preferred Explanation for 'Badness'

At the end of the last chapter we asked the question as to whether there exist any other instances, apart from in the field of addiction, where the notion of disease is used functionally to redefine types of behaviour which might otherwise be viewed in a negative light. In fact, such instances are not difficult to find. One example which occurs with some regularity involves petty theft, where this is perpetrated by a well-known or respected public figure. For example, not so many years ago the unfortunate Lady Barnett was involved in such an affair. Isabelle Barnett, a titled woman held in high regard by members of the public from all walks of life due to her attractive personality and wit on the television quiz 'What's My Line', seemed to most people an unlikely person to be involved in a shop-lifting scandal. Nonetheless, she was convicted of such an offence, and the affair attracted more attention than was warranted simply because she was in the public eye. It appears that Lady Barnett suffered high levels of psychological stress after the incident; in the event, she took her own life some time later in a tragic and grotesque manner. However, whatever the personal reasons behind her unfortunate death, her acts of theft were predictably attributed in contemporary media accounts to a 'condition'; whether this diagnosis helped or hindered Lady Barnett in coming to terms with her behaviour remains a matter for conjecture.

The condition known as kleptomania is defined in terms of a compulsive desire to steal not unlike the compulsive desire to gamble. Kleptomania is in fact very poorly documented; there is

74

little scientific evidence, other than psychiatric and other allegedly expert opinion, to distinguish between kleptomania and ordinary habitual stealing; a fact which mirrors the postulated distinction between heavy and compulsive gambling discussed in the previous chapter. The fact that firm evidence is lacking, however, is irrelevant since the function of the kleptomania label is not to mirror established scientific fact, but rather to make something easier to live with for the time being. Such a strategy, however, provides short-term social advantages at the expense of longer-term solutions, as we shall see later.

By way of contrast, when petty theft is committed by an archetypal 'villain', for example a twenty-year-old unemployed youth with a prior record of football hooliganism, vandalism, stealing or whatever, no one will be in a great hurry to suggest that he is 'suffering' from the 'condition' of kleptomania. The twist in the logic is startling; the 'disease' label is applied to the atypical event, whereas the chronic event is judged culpable. In a medical context, the same criterion would suggest that a single sneeze was pneumonia, whereas a lifetime of emphysema was culpable bad behaviour.

In fact, the medical label in this context has nothing to do with science, and everything to do with social expediency. There is no societal problem, once someone is defined as 'bad', in finding them guilty of doing bad things on purpose. When people socially defined as good do such things, however, a different kind of explanation is required; namely, one that removes the perceived culpability. Unhappily, this is only achieved at the price of imposing the associated and more permanent label 'mentally ill' or 'sick' upon the perpetrator, so there is thus a heavy price to pay in social terms for the absolution of sin by this means. One trades temporary badness for chronic illness.

In a previous chapter we have reasoned against the absurdity of defining entire, integrated sequences of purposive behaviour in terms of the involuntary symptomatology of a supposed disease. Such a definition, whilst meeting immediate social purposes, has unfortunate consequences. The futile search commences for the underlying mechanisms of the postulated disease, when what is required is an understanding of why the social world in which we live, and which we have created, leads a member of the aristocracy to display the same criminal behaviour as a twenty-year-old unemployed youth, and vice versa. By removing the acts of Lady

Barnett to a different causal plane, we make it that much less likely that we will come to a realistic and empathic understanding of either the problems of unemployed youth or of Isabelle Barnett, or of the interaction between shoplifting, individual motives, and the economic situation in general.

An even more striking example of 'pathologification' (the tendency to define ordinary, non-pathological bits of behaviour in terms of disease) comes from the wider psychological literature, and concerns reading difficulties particularly amongst children. It is well known that some people having specific and identifiable damage to parts of the central nervous system show accompanying perceptual and cognitive deficits, some of which take very striking forms. Some sufferers, for example, are unable to name everyday objects; others can identify everyday objects by feel with one hand, but not with the other; and others have perceptual problems when viewing certain types of figures, involving confusions with up-down orientation or lateral inversion. Such demonstrable deficits often have clear and indisputable implications for the reading and writing skills of the sufferer, and to the extent that this is the case the label 'dyslexia' is both diagnostically helpful and appropriate.

However, great importance is attached to the ability to read in modern societies, and it is hardly surprising that the label 'dyslexia' has come into everyday use as an explanation for why many children cannot read in a more general sense. It is interesting to examine more closely the way in which the definition of dyslexia has progressively broadened to take in more and more people with reading difficulties, including more and more individuals who do not show any signs of deficit other than difficulty with reading.

Dyslexia as Functional Explanation

Whilst there is argument about the precise mechanisms underlying dyslexia, the central notion is that sufferers from the condition fail to learn to read for reasons which are of constitutional origin. In other words, there is literally something wrong with the person, whether at the level of failure of normal development, stunted growth, specific brain dysfunction or whatever. Miles and Miles write (1983, p.2) 'that some kind of constitutional limitation is involved seems to us to be established beyond any reasonable doubt.'

This 'condition' notion of dyslexia is generally the most favoured amongst workers in this area, and several recent texts are available on the topic (e.g. Coltheart, Patterson and Marshall 1987; Quin and Macauslan 1988; Miles and Miles 1983 *op cit)*.

In the present text, however, we are primarily concerned with the insights provided by attribution theory, a central feature of the argument being that functionality is a feature of the attribution process; that is, we prefer modes of explanation that serve purposes for us. Bearing this in mind, the reader's attention is now drawn to the opening paragraphs (pp2-3) in the Miles and Miles book (*op cit*) which can be interpreted entirely as explanation which is functional rather than veridical. The authors write:

'In our view the actual word *dyslexia* is unimportant, since a word of approximately equivalent meaning would do as well, such as 'specific learning disability'. What is important is the orientation – the particular view of the child's difficulties – which use of the word implies.

It is sometimes said that parents and child are discouraged or demoralized when they are told that the child is dyslexic. In our experience this is almost never the case, at least if the word is properly explained to them. On the contrary they are often very much relieved (sic- author). The reason seems to be that when one gives parents information about typical cases of dyslexia this makes sense of what would otherwise have seemed extremely bewildering. . . . . . .and if one can make it clear that the child is suffering from a recognised disability. . . ..this makes it much easier for them to give the appropriate kind of support. Similarly, if teachers can be told, not, 'Here is yet another backward reader,' but rather, 'Here is a child *with a disability which requires special understanding,* it will be possible for them to help the child in a constructive way'.

The quoted paragraphs contain a number of frankly hair-raising ideas. First, there is the suggestion that teachers do not cope 'constructively' with backward readers, but only with those who suffer from a 'recognised disability', the reasoning behind which does not bear close examination. Is it the implication that backward readers do not deserve special understanding, whereas those 'suffering from' dyslexia do because 'it's not their fault'?

Furthermore, we see the actual word dyslexia has no special merit, other than that it cheers people up (they are 'very much relieved'), one of its major virtues being that it makes parents joyful to discover that their progeny's reading problems arise not due to childish indolence, lack of attention or interest or whatever, but because in some sense their child is defective or sick. Whilst this might help parents with their self-presentation problems in the short term, the effects of the label in the longer term remain a matter for speculation and concern.

Finally, just as treatment for alcohol and drug problems is conditional on acceptance of a 'sick' label, so it is apparently with reading difficulties. Better teaching, we are told, is only obtained in return for accepting the 'dyslexia' label. It remains simply to say that deals of this type are not necessarily beneficial in all cases, or in the long term.

All in all, Miles and Miles comments could not have been put better by an attribution theorist; and once again we see clearly how people prefer explanation in terms of mechanism when a high-value issue with moral overtones is involved. Failure to read is after all 'shameful', and any explanation offered has to address that problem and solve it.

When attribution theory works in this way, the bizarre situation arises in which the immediate family of the sufferer rejoices at the news of their loved one's infirmity.

Dyslexia; An Alternative View

In general terms, dyslexia refers to a situation in which a child of normal intelligence, (i.e. with normal performance on various other tasks, or even above-average performance) fails to learn to read. However, within the psychological literature there was at one time a heated debate about whether dyslexia referred to a specific identifiable state which is differentiated from mere reading difficulties; or whether in fact no such distinction exists. Some of these points were raised by Whittaker (1982) during a series of exchanges in the Bulletin of the British Psychological Society. Whittaker upset a number of people with statements like the following:

'It was with some dismay that I saw the announcement of one more international conference on causes, diagnosis and treatment of dyslexia . . . . The only justification for such a

gathering would be if the aim were to reach agreement about abandoning the term dyslexia from all literature, medical and educational.'

And later,

'Dyslexia is a hoax in need of thorough exposure. . . . .Dyslexia was and is a medical term without a sound scientific basis.'

Finally,

'It is hardly anything new that poor readers read with frequent fixations and regressive eye-movements, and previous research has firmly disclaimed such findings as decisive in the diagnosis of dyslexia. But in the 1980's in this country research grants are still going in the direction of efforts to prove the existence of the nebulous concept of dyslexia on such grounds'.

The debate still continues today, but perhaps in a less heated fashion.

Given these disagreements among the experts, it is permissible to entertain the argument that children fail to learn to do all sorts of things, and that the postulation of dyslexia in a specific case *may* have more to do with the societal value attached to reading than with the scientific defensibility of the definition. Failure to learn to read is symbolic in terms of social value in a way which goes far beyond failure, say, to make model aeroplanes or play hockey. Failure to read requires therefore to be explained in terms that make it easier to live with, and the main function of the dyslexia label is that it does exactly that.

It is a worthwhile exercise to consider the possible reasons why we have a medical condition called dyslexia; whereas there is no medical condition of 'velocoplexia' (inability to ride a bike) despite the fact that a highly convincing case could be made out for the latter based on minimal vestibular dysfunction. The reason is that parents are less sensitive to their children's inability to ride a bike than to their inability to read. Consequently, if dyslexia did not exist, it would be necessary to invent it; which is exactly what has happened according to Whittaker.

Returning now to the areas of 'addiction', 'alcoholism' and 'compulsive gambling' we can see that, regardless of whether disease explanations fit the facts or not, there are reasons supporting the use of these concepts which derive directly from societal values which are second nature, and which are rigorously defended. A crucial facet of 'addiction' which influences treatment offered, outcome success, and all aspects of the substance-abuse system, as well as the nature of the individual cognitions of sufferers, is that it involves behaviour which in terms of conventional societal values needs to be explained as malfunction. It *would* therefore involve the notion of guilt, for which punishment rather than treatment is generally felt to be appropriate; or worse imply that using drugs was a reasonable adaptation to the world in which we live, *should* an explanation be offered in terms of personal responsibility or voluntary action.

Addiction is thus driven by a moral, rather than a scientific, consensus. In the absence of such a moral consensus a particular kind of behaviour could not have attributed to it the features that are said to characterise, and that we require from, our addictions. And though people would still encounter the same problems deriving from what Orford (1985 *op cit*) terms their 'excessive appetites', there would be no such thing as 'addiction' *per se*.

8

The Nature of
the Evidence:
Methodological
Problems

In the light of the previous chapters, two questions naturally arise. These are, first, how does it come about that stereotyped perceptions of addiction continue to exert such a powerful influence, and what is the nature of the evidence which apparently supports such views? Secondly, what evidence exists to support the alternative view of addiction proposed here? The next two chapters address these questions, starting with a review of some common methodological problems.

The resources invested in answering 'people' problems are usually quite modest compared to the massive sums invested in tackling engineering and technological problems. A project in the 'people' area will typically cost the price of two salaries for two years work, involve a questionnaire and some computing, and will frequently rely entirely on people's verbal reports despite the fact that these have been repeatedly shown to be variable in important respects as well as context dependent. As a consequence, methodological innovation is stifled by shortage of funds, and progress hindered by the consequent inability to separate popular wisdoms from useful insights. In an age when we can put men on the moon, the answers to important questions such as 'How much do people drink?' or 'Does drug education actually work?' still regularly hinge around asking people for their verbal estimates, views and opinions. The resources necessary to answer such questions in a more satisfactory manner are generally not available, and consequently much social research appears to do little more than confirm a currently acceptable verbal consensus.

81

Bearing in mind these points, it is now proposed to examine three issues concerning the nature of the data commonly used to support propositions in the area of addiction. The first of these issues concerns reliance on verbal reports about the way the world *is*, and the failure to grasp the extent to which answers to questions are acts of cognitive construction rather than statements of some absolute 'truth'. Whilst asking questions may offer a route to understanding how people think about the world, it remains an unsatisfactory way of finding out how the world is. Nonetheless, many researchers continue to use verbal report data for the latter purpose without apparently being aware that a problem even exists.

Answers to Questions: True or False?

In the general psychological literature there is a mass of theoretical knowledge about question artefacts, interviewer effects, scale factors, adaptation levels and so forth; and in terms of analysis, there are powerful statistical tools for testing causal hypotheses provided data are collected in a manner which justifies their use. Yet there exist fields of applied research which have remained more or less untouched by such theoretical development, and this includes certain areas of the study of addiction. A major subset of the literature relies on questionnaire/interview data gathered in a theoretical vacuum and analysed by cross-tabulations. Government (OPCS) surveys of national drinking practices (Goddard 1986; Goddard and Ikin 1988; Knight and Wilson 1980; Wilson 1980; Dight 1976) are classic illustrations of this approach, and though they invariably achieve standards of excellence when viewed alongside other research of this type, they still rely on the atheoretical presentation of data of unknown validity. A more detailed review of the arguments concerning verbal reports can be found in two editorials to the *British Journal of Addiction* (Davies 1987 and 1989).

For the most part, answers to questions are viewed as a means of finding out the 'truth' about some situation or pattern of behaviour. In addition it is often assumed that people can report not merely what they did, but also 'why' they did it. An answer, it appears, gives a guide to the 'truth' subject to two sources of distortion, namely (i) memory may be less than perfect, and (ii) people may deliberately falsify their answers. Answers to questions thus reveal the 'truth' minus a component for faulty memory, minus a component for deliberate falsification. It is assumed that if one could eliminate these two sources of error one would be left with 'truth'.

This view is questioned by a growing body of evidence which suggests that answers are acts of cognitive construction rather than merely degraded versions of truth. It derives from the suggestion that the answers people give serve important functions for that person (e.g. self-presentation, preservation of self-esteem, apportioning credit or blame) and that the answers the person offers reveal first and foremost something about the way that person thinks, and about his/her motives and intentions, rather than merely providing a blurred window on the truth.

In many studies of prevalence, researchers have suggested that answers to 'use' questions generally tend to be underestimates. Since the validity of individual answers is unknown this assertion of universal under-reporting can be nothing more than an assumption. As such it derives from a consensual view that drug using is bad and therefore everyone will wish to underestimate the extent to which they do it. This may not be the case. For example, in 1972 Davies & Stacey produced a report on teenage alcohol consumption in which it was found that the consumption of alcohol was associated with (i.e. was seen as) being 'sociable-sexy' and 'tough-mature'. These dimensions have been found several times by other workers. In such circumstances, where these types of association exist, the consumption of alcohol clearly might have self-presentation value especially for those teenagers perceiving themselves as deficient in sociability-sex or toughness. For these people, self-presentation pressures may be towards over-reporting rather than under-reporting, since the heavy-drinking tough guy is potentially an attractive image. Whatever the truth of the matter, there is little theoretical justification for a blanket assumption that people will invariably under-report their 'bad habits'; the doers of these things may not even see the activity in those terms.

The assumption that the motivation to deliver other than the truth is removed by the simple assurance of anonymity also merits some scrutiny. Such a strategy only looks at one side of the coin and assumes a universal tendency to under-report stemming from a uniform negative evaluation of the activity; but as we have already noted there may not be such a uniformly negative consensus. The assumption is that because the researcher would be unhappy about publicly revealing that he/she did this thing, everyone else must feel the same. However the motive to produce accounts of the social world that protect self-esteem by over-reporting remains untouched by such elementary procedures; and being able to drink more than anybody else is in fact something of which people are often proud, and about which individuals will frequently boast. Although assurances of anonymity ensure that no outsider can marry up an answer set with a particular individual, the answers being provided are open to the scrutiny of the person doing the answering, and they have to be acceptable and make sense to him/her in the context of a particular social interaction with a particular type of interviewer or questionnaire.

A number of interesting artefacts were demonstrated in a paper by McKennel (1970), who reported the results from studies of the incidence of smoking amongst young people aged 11 to 16. Data were collected by a variety of methods, a procedure which permitted method-specific artefacts to be identified; something which is not possible where methods are standardised, and where any bias cannot consequently be detected. Factors found to increase self-reports of smoking included questionnaire self-completion rather than interviewer-completion; being interviewed at school rather than at home; and being interviewed in a class situation rather than individually. In addition, there were sex differences, with the effects generally failing to reach statistical significance for the girls, but being highly significant amongst the younger boys. Amongst the latter, there was a five-fold difference between reports obtained in the home as opposed to the classroom situation. Furthermore, the school v. home difference was not due to the presence or absence of parents in the home; home interviews were found to be uninfluenced by presence or absence of parents.

However, and contrary to the popular wisdom, an emphasis on the confidentiality of the interview produced a *decrease* in reporting rather than an increase; due McKennel suggests to the increase in the perceived sensitivity of the topic created by emphasising confidentiality. He writes, '. . .a heavy stress on confidentiality evidently arouses more mistrust than if this aspect is only lightly mentioned.' Finally, as might be expected, the inclusion of a repeated probe question about 'trying even one cigarette' increased the numbers admitting to regular smoking.

In conclusion McKennel states that 'prevalence estimates from studies of children's smoking are highly contingent, especially for the younger boys, on the method by which the data are obtained.' He then goes on to make an important point, that will be raised later. Even though the absolute levels of reported use cannot be considered either reliable or valid, correlations or other measures of association between reported smoking levels and other variables should remain unaffected by these biases, since the ordinal nature of the data is far more robust than the actual levels reported.

At a simpler level there are many instances in which answers to questions become straight substitutions for actual events. For example, recent evaluations of the success or otherwise of anti-drug-use campaigns on the television have made use of subject's perceptions of the likely impact of the material on the target populations. Or in plain English, people were asked to speculate about the likely effect of the drug education. Yet quite soon ministers and others were talking about the success of the campaigns rather than talking about people's guesses at the success of the campaigns. In fact, the recent National Evaluation of Drug Education in Scotland (Coggans *et al* 1990; 1991) clearly showed that whilst teachers and specialist drug-coordinators believed that recent drug education in schools was changing attitudes and altering drug-use behaviour, there was no evidence from those who received the education that either of these things had taken place.

In a similar fashion, a report on the impact of the more liberal licensing laws introduced in Scotland in 1976 relied heavily on people's opinions (Goddard 1986 *op cit*). Once again reports that many people thought it was a good idea become a stepping stone in the short path from thinking that something is a good thing, to something being a good thing, and the apparently logical development that therefore we should have more of it. In an analogous way within the addiction literature, reported reasons for relapse become the events that cause relapse; reports of consumption become the amounts consumed; and explanations for behaviour become the reasons that behaviour takes place.

Interviewer Effects

There is nothing new or novel about the suggestion that different interviewers and interviewing techniques have a marked impact on data collected. During the 1960s a number of classic studies emerged from a team at the Survey Research Centre. One of these (Belson *et al* undated; *circa* 1968) investigated self-reported theft by adolescent boys. The design of the study is of special interest, since it set out to achieve two sets of goals simultaneously. Namely, to find out something about theft, but also to find out something about the procedures and methods used in the investigation itself. Belson was interested in the impact of the method of eliciting the information, upon the information obtained. He used a variety of procedures, including casual and formal interviewers, sitting the interviewer behind a screen, eliminating the spoken word from the interview as far as possible by writing everything on cards, and ensuring that the boys were not spoken to by the interviewer outside the context of the interview. All in all, the interviewing procedure went through eight stages of development, after which Belson *et al* concluded that despite all precautions the quantitative accuracy of the verbal reports was still doubtful. Whilst their procedures produced indices of stealing that would be useful as discriminants in analysis, Belson concluded that the data were still open in absolute terms to an unknown degree of under- or over-reporting. Belson also makes the obvious but important point that procedural modification can improve the reliability of these kinds of data, but improved reliability gives no guide to validity. In other words, truth is unknowable by these means.

With respect to drug use, a clear interviewer effect was demonstrated in research by Ball (1967), which showed that drug users' answers to questions varied depending on the interviewer's familiarity with the drug sub-culture, and his/her institutional contacts. Stemming from this observation, we decided to conduct our own study into this issue, using the experiences of Belson and of Ball as a starting point. The basis of the study (Davies and Baker 1987) was an *ad hoc* questionnaire whose only virtue was that it contained a selection of the types of questions commonly used in questionnaires about drug use. Two versions of the questionnaire were produced, which asked the same questions using different words, to give two 'parallel forms'.

We located a sample of twenty heroin users in the East end of Glasgow to take part in the study. The main point of the experimental design was to assess the impact of using two contrasting styles of interviewer to collect the data, and to do this we first of all trained a 'straight' interviewer, who presented himself during the actual interviews as representing the Addiction Research

Group at Strathclyde University. The second interviewer was a drug user known to us in connection with other studies we were carrying out. He presented himself as having been recruited by 'the university' to 'help out with some interview stuff'.

The drug-using interviewer started by interviewing ten subjects about their drug involvement, using the first version of the questionnaire. He then interviewed the remaining ten using the second version. Between ten and fourteen days after their first interview, each respondent was visited again by the straight interviewer, who interviewed them again using the appropriate alternative form of the schedule. The results from this simple study are summarised in Table 1 below.

Table 1 Results of Significance Tests, and Measures of Association, between Data from the Two Interviewers

Question no.	Test	Significance	Tau	Significance
1.	*t*	$p<0.001$	0.66	$p<0.001$
2.	sign	$p<0.001$	0.65	$p<0.01$
3.	sign	$p<0.001$	0.43	$p<0.05$
4.	sign	$p<0.001$	0.49	$p<0.02$
5.	*t*	$p<0.001$	0.86	$p<0.001$
6.	sign	$p<0.001$	0.54	$p<0.01$
7.	*t*	$p<0.001$	0.55	$p<0.01$
8.		NS	0.80	$p<0.001$
9.	sign	$p<0.001$	0.54	$p<0.02$
10.	/	/	/	/
11.	/	/	/	/
12(a)	sign	$p<0.002$	0.19	NS
12(b)	sign	NS	0.44	$p<0.05$

The results in Table 1 can be divided into two subsets; first the results of significance tests, which indicate whether there were important differences between the data obtained by the two interviewers; and second, whether the two data sets were associated. As can be seen, the results of the significance tests indicate that answers on nine of the eleven scaleable variables differed. Looking at the overall picture, it is immediately apparent that the 'straight' interviewer received reports of heavier use, higher expenditure on drugs, heavier withdrawal symptoms, greater difficulty in 'coming off drugs', longer history of drug use, greater degree of 'addiction', and so forth. In a word, the straight man was presented with the junkie stereotype, whereas the picture presented to the known drug-using interviewer was less extreme. It is, of course, impossible to determine whether either picture is 'true'. More probably, both pictures are legitimate acts of construction which take into account the way the drug-user perceived the interviewer, and his perceptions of the type of information required. After all, when you talk to the doctor it is usually to tell him how sick you are, rather than to tell him that you are really quite well.

The second aspect of the data worth mentioning concerns the fairly high correlations between answer sets. Correlation does not mean 'same as' but refers to the ability to predict one thing from another. For example, the number series 1,2,3,4,5 correlates perfectly with the number series 1 million, 2 million, 3 million, 4 million, 5 million, even though there is a huge difference in actual magnitude. Thus, in the present study, the correlations indicate that to a considerable degree one set of results is predictable from knowledge of another, even though the two sets are significantly different. The fact that the sets are associated indicates that the results are systematic rather than random. In the present instance, it means that a heavy user (compared to the others in the sample) comes out as a heavy user to both interviewers, though the amounts he reports differ significantly on the two occasions. In statistical terms, this means that the ordinal characteristics of the data are more robust than the absolute values. Consequently, when reporting studies of the extent of drinking and drug-use, data should only be regarded as trustworthy in relative, rather than absolute terms.

Two points emerge from this discussion. Firstly, it has been known for two decades that answers to questions depend on the way the interviewee perceives the interviewer, and this is especially the case when the behaviour in question involves a moral dimension, like theft or illicit drug use.

Secondly, the ordinal characteristics of questionnaire data are more useful than the absolute values. In 1968, Jessor *et al* wrote on this topic, '. . . . ...it would be naive for either the researcher or the reader to accept the face value of the interview or test scores as wholly accurate representations of the amount of drinking and problem behaviour actually taking place . . . . If we make the assumption that the distorting effects of memory and self-protection have a roughly equal influence on all respondents, then we should at least be able to *order* the respondents fairly accurately. . . .'; and finally, 'The actual scores reported by the respondents are simply considered as *symbolic of* the extent of the particular behaviour being studied.'

Apart from a study by Davies and Stacey (*op cit*) which took heed of Jessor's comments, there is little evidence that the majority of alcohol and drug research carried out at the present time makes any concessions whatsoever to the fact that the results obtained from questionnaires and surveys cannot be separated from the people and methods employed in the study. Nor is there any marked hesitancy on the part of researchers to do other than regard their consumption data as 'true'. Treating data solely in terms of their ordinal characteristics, and conceding like Belson and Jessor that answers to questions are merely 'symbolic', or 'useful as discriminants in analysis,' is still virtually unheard of.

Consequently, a first response to the questions posed at the beginning of this chapter is that much of the data on addiction is of questionable validity, being for the most part collected by means that make little reference to established theory and method. Part of the problem seems to be that too many drug workers 'know' that their clients trust them, and tell them nothing but the truth. The much-abused term 'in depth' has come to mean 'truer'.

Retrospective Recall; Retrieval or Construction?

Researchers in addiction frequently have to rely on user's reports about things that happened to them in the past, so it is worthwhile examining the properties of memory for events. 'Memory' data are particularly important in research which tries to find links between fluctuations in substance use and periods of calm or turmoil in people's lives; and also in investigations into developmental aspects of addiction which require information about the early stages of the process, or about early as opposed to later symptoms.

It is an established fact, demonstrated many times over the past fifty years, that memory is imperfect, selective and interpretive, and there is no reason to suppose that these characteristics of memory disappear simply because the topic is addiction and the interviewer is, say, a clinical psychologist. For example, a well known paper by Hastorf and Cantril (1954) entitled 'They Saw a Game' describes the recollections of a group of people who watched the same game of American football. The nature of their recollections, which included quantitative information such as the number of fouls committed by the two teams as well as descriptions of the match, were inaccurate, and biased according to which team they supported. The article contains material of fundamental importance for the understanding of recollection, and also of attitudes at a more general level, which normally goes unheeded in addiction research. Namely:

> '. . . .an 'occurrence' on the football field or in any other social situation does not become an experiential 'event' unless and until some significance is given to it. . . ..'and also:

'An attitude would seem to be a complex of registered significances reactivated by some stimulus which assumes its own particular significance for us *in terms of our purposes*'. (my italics). In other words, memory is not simply a hot line to the events of the past; that is, a simple way of finding out what actually happened. It is functional for the person doing the remembering, and its nature is shaped by the functions it serves.

Other examples illustrating the fact that memory is more than simple recollection of things that happened are commonplace. For example, the game based on 'Chinese Whispers', where a message is relayed from person to person, eventually produces a message that emerges in a totally unrecognisable form as people re-interpret what they think they heard. A similar effect was demonstrated in the classic study by Bartlett (1932) which involved the sequential copying of a drawing. The drawing became transmuted from an owl-like figure into a cat as people imposed their own experience onto the material they were trying to remember.

In studies of the development of drinking behaviour, almost without exception, the issue of age of first drink arises in some form. Respondents will be asked in one way or another to report the age at which they first had some experience of alcohol, and subsequently this reported age will be used in analysis, usually to argue the toss as to whether earlier experience is associated with heavier consumption in later life.

In the 1972 study of Teenagers and Alcohol (Davies and Stacey *op cit*) respondents were asked to report age of first drink. Subsequent analysis revealed that answers to this question were correlated with age of the respondent, older respondents reporting that they were older at age of first drink. By and large, 14-year-olds said they were about 9 or 10 years old when they had their first drink, 15 year olds said about 11 or 12, and sixteen and seventeen-year olds said about 13 or 14. In the 1976 study of Ten-to-Fourteen-year-olds and Alcohol

(Aitken 1976) a similar question was asked, and the same thing was found. In an analysis of variance of these data, two main effects were found, one for age and one for sex. Of these two, the main effect for age was highly significant (p<.001), greatly exceeding the magnitude of the effect for sex. The effect showed that reported age of first drink was principally a function of age of the respondent. Aitken writes,'. . . .in other words, the older children tended to say that they had the first drink they could remember tasting at a later age than did the younger children. . .'. Finally, in a study for the Scottish Home and Health Department, Hammersley, Morrison, Davies and Forsyth (1989 *op cit*) looked at alcohol and drug use amongst samples of drug users in and out of prison. As before, the question about age of first use was raised, and analysed by means of regression. This form of analysis showed that, once again, reported age of first use predicted the age of the respondent better than it predicted anything else. Taken together, these three pieces of evidence, collected in different ways and analysed by different statistical means, reveal conclusively that this question is quite different in nature from its surface appearance. Although it looks as though it measures age of first drink or first drug-use, it actually functions much better as a guide to how old the person is.

The first question now arises as to the meaning of all those studies which use self-reports of age of first use as an independent variable against which to classify other drug or alcohol-related behaviours. A second question arises from the fact that whilst this particular question now has a research history, and its nature is understood, the majority of other block-booked questions in typical questionnaire studies have not been examined in detail. How many other 'standard' questions operate in a similar artifactual manner? The second question is not answerable in the absence of specific data. However, in response to the first question, we can see that the item about age of first use is a bad one because it makes assumptions about how people 'remember'. Drinking and drug use are processes that start from zero and rise progressively over time in a continuous manner. Drinking does not suddenly 'switch on' at some point in time. Consequently, even with the best will in the world, there are real difficulties in deciding what to count as the 'first drink' or the 'first taste', or what to count as the 'beginning'. So the question deals not with 'fact' but with selection of a criterion for response. People simply do not know when it 'started', any more than they know when they started to 'play football' or 'go shopping'. Given these circumstances, people will make the best of a bad job by providing a symbolic answer, since that is all that is available to them. In the absence of any specific memory, they provide something that seems reasonable. The result is a question which functions systematically, and which therefore will meet all the statistical criteria relating to consistency, but which measures something quite different from that which it is assumed to measure.

Furthermore, from this viewpoint, we might also hypothesise that heavier users would report earlier use, especially if they are experiencing problems, because it makes sense for them to do so in the circumstances and in the absence of any clear recollection. On this topic, it is instructive to refer to a recent study of drinking habits carried out in New Zealand by Casswell *et al* (1990). The study is interesting because it compares people's early and later drinking, employing a longitudinal design that involved collecting data every second year, from a group of some 1,000 children born between 1972 and 1973. In this study, data on alcohol consumption were collected from boys and girls at ages 9,11,13 and 15 years. Caswell *et al* start by citing results from a number of studies (Gonzalez 1983; Friedman and Humphrey 1985; Barnes and Welte 1986), all of which conclude that earlier drinking predicts heavier consumption in later life, on the basis of retrospective recall of earlier drinking. We may note from the outset that an artifact should clearly be anticipated in these circumstances; heavier drinking *now* may obviously have an impact on a person's reports of their earlier drinking due to a simple cognitive-consistency or 'halo' effect. Once again, this suggestion is neither new nor radical, and the effect has been well established in the broader psychological literature. Work by Conway and Ross (1984) and Ross (1989) shows how people reconstruct the events of the past so as to make more sense of the present. In the former of these studies, for example, a group of people who participated in a study-skills training programme that was of limited effectiveness, subsequently rated their prior level of competence as lower than was actually the case. Conway and Ross conclude that their results support the hypothesis that people 'claim support for invalid theories of change by reconstructing their pasts,' and Ross suggests that 'people often rely on implicit theories for their reports of long-term, personal memories.'

Returning to the study in hand, Casswell *et al* report correlations between levels of reported consumption at the different ages and conclude: 'However, the correlations were still fairly small, imply-ing that the ability to predict the level of drinking at a later age, given it at a younger one, is not very good.' And later: 'Tracing the movement of the heaviest drinkers also illustrates the same pattern. Of those in the heaviest drinking top 10%, about one in five were still in the top 10% two years later. Four years later, this had dropped to about 15%.' (i.e. roughly one in seven – author)

Once again, we see how results obtained depend on method, retrospective recall providing a picture of greater drinking consis-tency over time than is revealed by time-sampled data. The clear implication is that such consistency comes from the subjects themselves, and that from an attributional perspective the emphasis on greater consistency makes for a more plausible explanation in circumstances where the 'truth' is not actually recalled.

Similar problems arise when subjects are asked to recall symptoms of drug or alcohol misuse; an important issue since certain diagnostic procedures make use of such recollections. If a person is asked a question about a past event and they respond in some way, we tend to assume they have 'remembered' it. Not 'remembering' is signalled by words such as 'I cannot remember'; any other response is evidence of 'memory'. Furthermore, a verbal statement about an event and a time is often taken to be evidence of memory conceptualised in terms of what is sometimes referred to as 'the deep freeze analogy'. According to this model, memories are stored away for years, like joints of meat in a freezer. Upon command, one opens the lid and hunts around inside for the object in question, subsequently a)finding it, or b)failing to find it by not looking properly ('I want you to go over the events again, and *try harder* to remember what the man in the car was wearing' says the policeman to the witness of a crime) or c)failing to find it because it was never there. In fact, memory is never like that in any literal sense; there are no objects in the brain. Memory is always an act of construction, and the extent to which it represents some consensual view of past reality depends on a variety of factors including the demand characteristics of the study and the motivational state of the person doing the remembering. In circumstances where there is no escape for the person being questioned, repeated questioning will eventually produce some act of construction, since there is in fact very little alternative for the person on the receiving end. Just as the eyewitness will be pressured to 'recall' something more, and plumb depths of deeper and deeper uncertainty, so the drug abusing patient finds him/herself in a situation where memories of events are required, and escape seems to be contingent on producing something regardless of its subjective degree of certainty, or shifts in the criterion for classifying the event as significant.

The phenomenon is illustrated in a paper by Anderson, Aitken and Davies (1981) in which people with alcohol problems were asked to recall their symptoms, and their order of occurrence. The method stems from earlier work which held promise from a diagnostic point of view, since high levels of concordance (agreement) were obtained from the patients (Chick and Duffy 1979). The crucial part of this earlier study involved the alcohol patients examining a list of symptoms of alcohol dependence, and rank-ordering these in terms of their order of occurrence. The results showed a high degree of consensus, indicating therefore a kind of developmental aspect to alcohol problems. The patients, remember, were asked to recall the ordering of their symptoms, and they complied by producing rank orderings. In our replication study, the initial experiment was repeated and produced very similar results. The only addition to the study was the inclusion of a second group of subjects, screened so as to eliminate anyone with an alcohol problem or any alcohol-related symptomatology. This group, with no first-hand experience, were asked to pretend that they were in treatment for alcohol problems, and then required to do the same task. Clearly, they could not recall a full rank-ordering of symptoms because these had never happened to them. Nonetheless, *they were able to comply with the task requirements without difficulty, and produced the same rank-ordering of symptoms as the real patients.*

The study shows that, asked to carry out a 'memory' task, a group with little or nothing to remember can readily comply with the instructions; and furthermore, that their results are indistinguishable from what we might erroneously describe as 'the real thing'. The argument that one set of results were real, while the others were merely 'making it up', shows a profound misunderstanding of the nature of memory, where what you get depends on what you ask, how you ask it, and the demand characteristics of the situation. Memories are always acts of construction at some level. Within the present context, given that sufferers from alcohol problems have difficulties with memory tasks, it is entirely reasonable to suggest that in fact both groups carried out the task in the same way. That is, in response to the demands of the study, they searched for and found a common criterion for carrying out the task: namely, the least-serious-looking symptoms come early on, and the more-serious looking ones come later.

People's Propensity to Make Sense of Their Lives

In 1958, Stott carried out a study into the aetiology of Down's Syndrome. His results led him to conclude that socio-emotional factors were important in causing the condition. Given that it is now known that the syndrome has a chromosomal basis, it is instructive to examine the procedures used by Stott that led him to conclude that life-stress during pregnancy was an important causal agent.

Basically, he asked mothers of Down's Syndrome children to recall life-events occurring during pregnancy, and compared their responses to those obtained from a comparable sample of mothers of normal children. The Down's Syndrome mothers reported more stressful events (i.e. reported experiencing more events as stressful) than did the control mothers.

This illuminating study poses two questions. Firstly, why did the method produce such apparently clear differences between the two groups in terms of reported stressful life-events? Secondly, how many other studies of life stress involve the same artifact, which goes undetected simply because an alternative mechanism has not yet been discovered?

What can we suggest by way of answer to the first of these questions? Explanations based on the assumption that mothers of Down's syndrome children are particularly prone to fantasy and invention, or uniquely afflicted by bad luck in all areas of their lives, simply do not make much sense; but two cognitive explanations seem to offer possibilities. The first suggests that, in the light of some negative outcome, people will re-interpret parts of their lives associated with that negative outcome in more negative terms. That is, they will come to see certain periods as 'bad times'. The second possibility is that a shorter-term effect is operating, whereby the subject of the experiment starts to make subjective sense of the experimental situation. When questioned about stressful events during pregnancy, the Down's syndrome mothers would react in an 'I see what he's driving at' type of manner; and perhaps start to think that, 'now he's mentioned it', there was quite a lot that went wrong during that period. In other words, the re-interpretation takes place in response to the questions being asked.

It seems very reasonable to suggest that the Down's Syndrome mothers had a good reason for finding more stressful events, because they had experienced something which required to be explained. The line of questioning implicitly offered a way of 'making sense of' a very distressing event, a way of finding an acceptable explanation.

The second question, concerning the extent to which such a process affects research in other areas, cannot be specifically answered, but it may be noted that much of the literature on life-events and addiction appears in principle to be open to this artefact, as well as being flawed on other ways. Lack of a testable theory, lack of adequate control groups, and uncritical reliance on retrospective memory are regular features of this body of literature. A more detailed critical review is available in O'Doherty and Davies (1987).

The principal point arising from the above illustration is that people will find reasons that enable them to make sense of their lives. These reasons are thus functional constructions, but in research we frequently treat reasons and causes as though they were much the same thing. In fact, reasons are produced by people to explain and make sense of their behaviour to themselves and others, whilst causes imply something that actually makes be-haviour happen. Sometimes, a stated reason and a cause may coincide, but where a morally disapproved of behaviour is concerned they are frequently different. A certain amount of addiction research treats reasons, which are psychological con-structs, as if they were causes. It is assumed too readily that i) people have direct access to the causes of their own behaviour, and ii)that the reasons they offer for their actions will be representations of those causes, rather than constructions whose function is to re-define the behaviour in question. In this way, the difference between the physical nature of causality, and the psychological nature of reasons, fails to impinge on the research. For example, in earlier studies of relapse by Litman *et al* (1977;1979) it is apparent that the reasons given by subjects were assumed by the authors to be primarily veridical and causal.

In the same way that psychologists and others sometimes ask subjects to remember things that, due to their progressive nature, cannot be remembered in the form requested, there is also an assumption that people do things for simply communicable reasons, and all that is necessary is to ask them to say what those reasons are. In fact, drug use is not an isolated behaviour but has all the characteristics of an integrated way of life; almost a career. Consequently, asking 'Why do you use drugs?' or 'What made you relapse?' are not questions to which there is an easy answer, especially one that fits nicely into a questionnaire format. One might as well ask someone, 'Why are you a chartered accountant / trapeze artist / concert pianist?' or whatever, pausing perhaps only to give them a check-list and instruct them to 'Tick One'.

There is seldom one simple primary reason underlying a career or vocation, but that seems to be what is sometimes required. The interesting aspect of this line of research, however, is not that it reveals the causes of behaviour, but that the kind of explanation the person *chooses to give* can reveal something about how they think, and what they make of themselves and of the researcher. There is now a growing literature on the ways in which drug-user's explanations vary as a function of pattern and type of drug use, and this is an issue we shall return to in a later chapter in the context of attribution theory. However, for the time being a single example will suffice to illustrate how coherent and replicable patterns of explanation arise which nonetheless are constructions rather than recollections of actual life events.

Classic work on the relationship between life-events and illness, particularly depression, has been carried out by Brown (1974) and Brown and Harris (1978). The method these authors have devised is certainly the most developed and intricate approach to the problem so far, but nonetheless the basic fact that data cannot be viewed independently of the method used to elicit them is still elegantly illustrated. The Brown and Harris method certainly produces cleaner data than some other methods, in the sense that it attempts to take into account context effects at a level not previously achieved, and controls for certain sources of bias. The method hinges on ratings of the impact of events made by the research team, rather than by the individual concerned. That is, the subject's memory for the timing and occurrence of events is permissable data, but his/her memory of the effect of the events is specifically excluded. If this procedure is followed, the data obtained are sometimes more useful as 'discriminants in analysis' than are data derived by other methods.

The fact remains, however, that unless the 'memory' data are collected according to Brown and Harris' method, one is unlikely to confirm Brown and Harris' hypotheses. At the end of the day, whether data collected by Brown and Harris method are true remains unknown and unknowable. There is a tendency sometimes to assume that a particular method is the 'right' one for all life-events research, because it confirms more hypotheses. Indeed, other workers who have elicited 'memories' in different ways and come up with different results (e.g. Schmid, Scharfetter, and Binder 1981) are sometimes castigated for not using the 'correct' method (see for example Brown and Harris 1982). The fact is, however, that results from these types of studies do not exist in a vaccuum, but only in the context of a particular research approach. In particular, the criterion for recall is very much a function of the instructions given to subjects. The 'deep freeze' analogy, by contrast, suggests that memories are stored somewhere in their entirety, and all you have to do is ask people to pull them out. If this were the case, the same results would obtain more or less indepedent of research method.

An interesting feature of the recall of events that have happened in the past is the phenomenon of 'fall-off'. In the simplest terms, this refers to the fact that the further back in time one goes, other things being equal, the fewer events are remembered (*other things being equal* refers to the fact that certain monolithic events and their timing remain permanent features of the record e.g. the death of a spouse at Xmas, and so forth). The basic problem is described by a number of workers but a succinct account comes from a paper by Jenkins, Hurst and Rose (1979), who write:

> 'Studies of life event recall that have addressed themselves to the forgetting hypothesis have reached quite different conclusions. These differences seem explainable in terms of the methods used. Generally, those studies that have concluded that recall of life events is not eroded by time are based on data collection at a single occasion and analysis of the trendline of events reported. In contrast, those studies that on two occasions have gathered data regarding the same period of time or those studies that have gathered data on one occasion but were able to verify it with documentation external to the respondent have quite consistently found substantial and progressive under-reporting for longer periods of recall. The reason for the discrepancy between these two types of studies is not immediately clear, but the greater methodological strength of

the latter type leads us to take seriously the problem of the forgetting of life events. This is particularly prominent for those events not involving major crises. Thus, the present findings raise a question about the validity of life stress and health change studies whose conclusions are based on trends of total life changes recalled from periods greater than nine months distant. This is particularly true when parallel longitudinal data from a control group are not available.'

The quote makes a number of points, two principal ones being that the picture emerging depends on whether you carry out 'one off' studies rather than a series of re-interviews; and the absence of data on recall of life-events from control groups, which latter omission characterises most of the research into life-events and addiction.

In a study of life events and problem use of tobacco, alcohol and illicit drugs (O'Doherty 1988; O'Doherty and Davies 1988 *op cit*), a semi-structured interview was devised, taking account of the procedures recommended by Brown and Harris (*op cit*), but with the exception that subjects themselves also provided ratings of the perceived impact of life events. Three groups of people with alcohol, tobacco and drug problems respectively took part in the study, and for each group a matched control group was selected from a larger pool of non-problem users, creating six groups in all. Certain relationships were found between changes in substance use and the perceived impact of events, and the main findings have been reported elsewhere (O'Doherty and Davies *op cit*; Davies 1990). However, the psychological nature of people's accounts of their lives was revealed when the memory-for-events data were examined more closely.

Each subject was interviewed on several occasions, at three-monthly intervals; the majority of subjects being interviewed five times over a fifteen-month period, with a few receiving a sixth interview at eighteen months. On each occasion, detailed information was sought about stressful events that were seen as affecting current behaviour, and which had occurred during the last three months. When histograms were plotted, showing number of recalled events against month of reported occurrence, a clear artifact emerged which is illustrated in the six figures below in Fig. 4.

It is apparent that subjects tended to report significant events as occurring principally in the weeks immediately preceding the current interview. This is revealed by the peaks in all graphs at

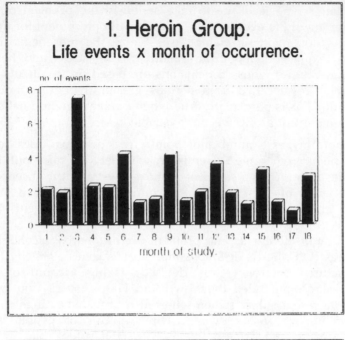

1. Heroin Group.
Life events x month of occurrence.

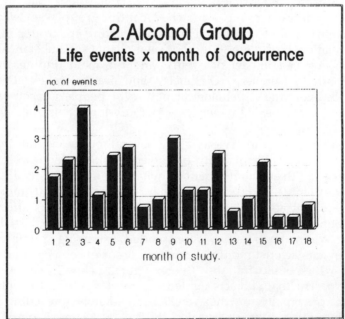

2. Alcohol Group
Life events x month of occurrence

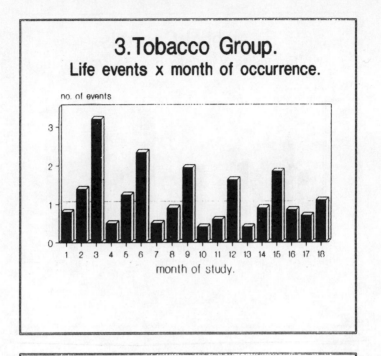

3.Tobacco Group.
Life events x month of occurrence.

no. of events

month of study.

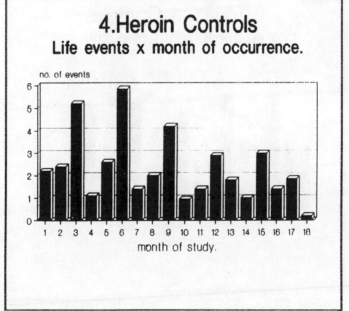

4.Heroin Controls
Life events x month of occurrence.

no. of events

month of study.

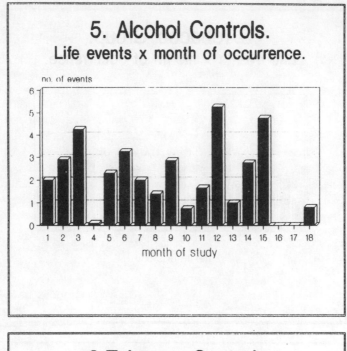

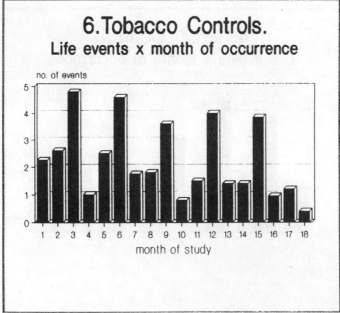

months 3,6,9,12,15, and to a lesser extent 18; that is, in the period immediately prior to each contact. More important, however, the artifact is shown to be procedural, rather than a due to some specific deficiency in the reporting of events by those with substance-abuse problems. All groups, including controls, show the same pattern.

It seems likely that, after a person has reported and exhausted their limited repertoire of major negative events (for example, the death of a spouse at Xmas) the interviewing procedure leads people to report events of progressively decreasing significance, simply because the procedure implies that they should do so. Consequently, events are eventually reported which do not in fact have any great significance other than the fact that have been recalled in response to the study; and because these events are generally less memorable, most of them tend to be of fairly recent origin. Nonetheless, on being later questioned about the impact of these events, subjects 'make sense of' their lives by relating any changes in substance use to the events they have reported, simply because it is the obvious thing to do within the context of the study.

Finally, in the discussion of whether this or that method of recall produces the 'most truth', the addiction worker is reminded that in other areas of psychology, the fact that the results obtained cannot be considered independently of the methods used to obtain them has been accepted and taken as standard practice for decades. In the area of psychophysics, for example, the laws relating perception to physical measures of reality only hold within a given methodology. A classic and widely-quoted paper by Poulton (1968), and a recent book (Poulton 1989) present findings of fundamental importance, but offer a species of argument which has so far not been mentioned within the addiction literature. Furthermore, the verbal recall of life events is partly a question of deciding *what* to select, that is, a decision-theory problem; and the standard literature on Decision Theory (e.g. Green and Swets 1966) clearly indicates the importance of differentiating the criterion for response from other factors.

In a typical signal-detection experiment, for example, subjects are asked to state whether some perceptual event (a flash of light; a sound; a change of some kind) has taken place or not. In a very loose sense, and at some risk, this can be conceptualised as a type of life-events research where the events are trivial perceptual changes, and the time scale for recall is very short. In such experiments, decision theory has shown the necessity of separating the detectability of a stimulus from the criterion for response. These two components are then used in order to describe a receiver-operating-characteristic (ROC) for each subject. There is no doubt that detectability and criterion together give a far better description of the probability that a subject in an experiment will (or will not) report seeing a light which has recently flashed, or hearing a brief sound which was presented (or whatever), than any of the 'classic' theories which assume the likelihood of detection to be primarily a function of stimulus strength. The criterion level depends on the motivational state of the subject, which is in turn a function of such things as past experience, expectations, perceived costs and benefits, and the instructions given by the experimenter. Further-more, criterion is separated from detectability by *varying* the rewards and costs, the instructions given, and other aspects of the experiment at each of a number of stimulus levels. At the end of the day, one can then describe (and *only* describe) the detectability of the stimulus relative to specified criterion levels (and also in the presence of a specified amount of 'noise'). Stimulus detectability is thus meaningless in the absence of some statement about criterion.

Remembering events, also, is not just a matter of 'detecting past events', but of establishing a criterion for reporting or not reporting them. Whether an event gets reported or not is similarly a function of the motivational state of the subject, perceived costs and benefits, expectations, and the instructions given, and not merely dependent on the 'importance' of the event. However, whilst the decision-theorist seeks to obtain an independent measure of criterion, it remains an uncontrolled variable as far as most life-events research is concerned. What exactly does the interviewer mean by a 'significant event'? Are my significant events the same as anyone else's? What are the risks involved in telling him/her about this? And what level of certainty is required here?

Criterion remains an uncontrolled variable which contributes to many of the problems arising in studies using retrospective recall and particularly life-events work. It is worth noting that psycho-physical methods have been successfully employed in attitude research, especially with respect to the validation of attitude-measurement scales; and with modification certain of the principles underlying signal detection theory might usefully be imported into the social domain with a view to establishing a more sensitive understanding of verbal recall for life events, should anyone wish to undertake the task. Specifically, the understanding of shifts in the *social criteria* for responding would appear to be a central issue when dealing with retrospective verbal reports.

In the meantime, we remain at a level of functioning where it is necessary to assume that an event took place if someone says it did, and did not take place if they say it didn't. The psychophysicist, operating at the same minimal level, would have to assume that a light flashed when someone said it did, and did not flash when they said it didn't. The whole point about decision theory, however, is that it explains how an individual comes to report a light flashing when no light flashes; and fails to report a light flashing when others are shielding their eyes. In the meantime, life-events research remains fixed at a surface level, with the consequence that the best current explanation is perhaps the one offered here; namely, people's recall for events appears to be characterised by, and modified by, a search for meaning, a desire to 'make sense' of their lives in the accounts they give. In decision theory terms, however, the question is more challenging, but also more capable of leading to a helpful answer. Namely, *what is the relationship between shifts in the criterion levels people adopt, and the circumstances they find themselves in?* Understanding how, and under what circumstances, people shift their criterion for responding in the *social* domain is one of the keys to developing a new paradigm for dealing with verbal reports at a deeper and ultimately more satisfying level. It is suggested that the idea of 'functional attribution' is a first clumsy step in that direction.

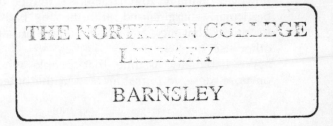

9

Attribution: A Dynamic Approach to How People Explain Their Actions

In the last chapter, we addressed the first of two important issues; namely, what methodological problems are encountered when using verbal behaviours to investigate addiction problems, and how method-specific artifacts might contribute to misleading results. In this chapter we address the second issue; namely, what light can be shed on people's verbal self-reports from an attribution theory standpoint, which sees explanation as deriving from the interaction of personal motives with social contextual cues, rather than as being in principle primarily veridical.

Attribution and the Expurgation of Guilt

A cornerstone of our everyday thinking is the habitual link between what we enjoy and what we believe is morally 'right'. For reasons which are specifically cultural, we tend to feel a need to 'prove' that the things we like to do are morally justifiable (e.g. fishermen are more likely to argue that fish do not feel pain), and we are unhappy if anyone suggests otherwise. There is also a contrary impulse however; namely to characterise things done by other people, particularly marginalised minorities, as 'bad' and to collect evidence to 'prove' that fact; and again we are unhappy if anyone suggests otherwise.

We habitually assume that people who do 'bad' things 'on purpose' deserve punishment. On the other hand, people who do 'bad' things may also be seen as deserving help provided that the act is attributable to circumstances beyond their control i.e. they did not do it 'on purpose'. In a sense, this simple attributional quasi-logic provides the basis for our legal system, where the basic task of the prosecution is to demonstrate that something 'bad' is done 'on purpose'.

The function of the addiction concept, which it holds in common with Jellinek's definition of alcoholism (1960), is to ensure that something we define as 'bad' is not also seen as done 'on purpose'. This grants permission for us to offer help rather than punishment, but it also recasts the doer of the 'bad' thing in the role of helpless victim. This has certain paradoxical consequences in the area of addiction. For example, drug dealing is seen as 'voluntary' and thus must be punished, whilst drug using is seen as 'forced' and thus merits 'treatment,' despite the fact that at the street level these two phenomena are inextricably interwoven (see Hammersley, Morrison, Davies and Forsyth 1989 *op cit*), most people involved with drugs taking part in both activities to some degree.

Three fundamental changes in thinking have to take place before we can make progress in dealing with drug problems. Firstly, we have to realise that it is not necessary to 'prove' that everything we do and enjoy is right or morally defensible; nor that things we do not do are 'bad'. Moral judgements of this type are always relative and a product of the time and place where they are made, and thus primarily reveal things about the society that makes them rather than about the activity in question. Secondly, people do not have to be 'good' or 'blameless' in order to deserve help. And finally, the categorisation of a particular piece of behaviour as 'good' or 'bad' does not have any logically necessary link to the perception of that behaviour as voluntary or non-voluntary; existing links being primarily socially functional insofar as they imply credit on the one hand or blame on the other.

Attributional 'Verdicts'

Recent work in the area of attribution has revealed a second level to the attributional process. Attributions about causality are aften accompanied by, or followed by, attributions about responsibility, particularly in the sense of 'Whose fault is it?'. This kind of thinking carries implications of blame and blamelessness, or in quasi-legal terms, of guilt and innocence. Once a person has proceeded thus far, they tend to entertain ideas as to what the appropriate dispensation ought to be in terms of either punishment or help. The idea of volition is central to this process, since in order to deserve punishment, something 'bad' has to be carried out 'on purpose'.

These kinds of second-order theories we shall refer to by the general term *attributional verdicts*, the general principles of which are easily illustrated by referring again to the Tom-hits-Mary illustration (see chapter 1). It will be remembered that high consistency, low consensus and low distinctiveness represented a set of circumstances leading to an explanation in terms of negative dispositional characteristics of Tom. On this basis, it is argued, there is a strong tendency to go one step further and apportion blame. In this case, the result is a characterisation of Tom as guilty and Mary as innocent. Furthermore, to the extent that Tom is seen is being the instigator of his own actions (i.e. he is not suffering from some 'disease' which makes him unable to control what he does) he is seen as deserving punishment. Mary, on the other hand, is globally characterised as 'helpless victim', and therefore as deserving of our help. Furthermore, the global label 'innocent' is readily attached to Mary in the absence of any information about her actual behaviour or intentions, and the question 'Innocent of what?' does not apply.

In an analogous way the unfortunate victims of a terrorist bomb attack on an aircraft will be characterised as innocent victims whilst guilt resides entirely with the terrorist. In circumstances such as these, the terms guilt and innocence do not indicate any specific guilt or innocence (i.e. the question 'Innocent of what?' again does not apply) but merely that the particular behaviour of the one party was judged bad and volitional, whilst that of the other was not-bad and/or not-volitional, the 'verdict' being made by some interested outside party.

Translating this into the language of addiction, we encounter the notion of the evil pusher, whose behaviour is bad and volitional (leading to the verdict 'guilty') and who is accordingly sent to prison; and the helpless addict, whose behaviour is bad but non-volitional ('not guilty') who is sent for treatment. In fact, users are generally actively involved to varying degrees in the processes of obtaining and distributing drugs, so the attributional polarisation between the active pusher and the helpless junkie victim is largely false in the real world. Consequently, from the drug users point of view the whole system must appear somewhat whimsical, since whether one falls foul of a prison sentence or a period of treatment is very much a matter of chance.

The idea of *attributional verdicts* is not new or revolutionary, and Fincham and Jaspars (1980) have proposed that from an attributional standpoint people are not so much naive scientists as naive lawyers, since attributions about responsibility are as common as attributions about causes. Indeed Shaver (1985) has produced a text entirely devoted to the attribution of blame which is relevant to these issues. Unfortunately, the research evidence on 'perceived responsibility' does not always provide clear guide-lines in a practical sense, due in part to a failure to take into account certain properties of the responsibility concept. The actual word 'responsible' has two facets; it may be taken to imply nothing more than causal agency (in the sense that clouds are responsible for rain); but it may also be used to infer fault or blame. Thus, though both drivers in a two-car crash are 'responsible' in a causal or philosophical sense (i.e. the particular crash would not have occurred in the absence of either of the participants), the admission of 'responsibility' by either party amounts in another sense to an admission of guilt, with the implication that the other driver had nothing to do with it. These and other conceptual difficulties have been investigated by Brewer (1977). Nonetheless, it is clear that in specific real-life situations, attributions of responsibility carry with them a freight of guilt-and-innocence and this is particularly marked where a strong moral consensus in terms of good v. bad prevails, as is the case with illicit drug use.

We have seen how ideas of responsibility, guilt and punishment are related. However, the opposite side of the coin also appears from time to time, insofar as judgements of lack-of-responsibility are related to ideas of innocence, and thence to the judgement that the individual is deserving of help. With respect to addiction, oblique support for this line of thinking is provided by research evidence from a completely different area of psychology, namely 'helping behaviour'. A field of study pioneered by Latane and Darley (1970) sought to discover the circumstances under which people would, or would not, offer assistance to each other in an emergency. Furthermore, some of the studies carried out included alcohol as a variable. For example, in a series of studies by Piliavin, Rodin and Piliavin (1969) an experimental stooge collapsed on the floor of a New York subway train and lay motionless. An observer recorded how many people came to the victim's aid, how long it took for help to be offered, and various other data. A number of variables were investigated, including the effect of racial difference between the victim and the possible helpers, with predictable results. However, in one condition the victim carried either i) a walking stick, or ii) a liquor bottle and smelled of drink. Victims carrying the stick received significantly more help than victims who were 'drunk'. Amongst the authors' conclusions is the following:

> 'An individual who appears to be ill is more likely to receive aid than is one who appears to be drunk, even when the immediate help needed is of the same kind.'

So much for alcoholism as disease! The authors' conclusions only make sense if 'drunk' is never a subset of 'ill'. More importantly, the study illustrates how perception of illness is a prerequisite to the offering of aid; and reveals the motivation behind Jellinek's well-known suggestion that alcohol misuse stemmed from a disease of alcoholism. It is apparent that Jellinek was intuitively aware of the attributional penalties of excessive alcohol use conceptualised in terms of a 'bad x volitional' interaction. By designating the problem as 'disease' he hoped to reclassify it as non-volitional, and thereby liberate treatment agencies and others to offer constructive help rather than a moral message (see Heather and Robertson, *op cit*). Specifically, *only if alcohol abuse is defined as illness are we able to bring ourselves to help those with alcohol problems.*

That is also the principle function of the concept of 'addiction'. It represents a re-classification which is necessary because as a society we appear to have difficulty with the idea of offering help to people whom we believe do not deserve it. 'Addiction' gives us permission to help people we see as 'bad'.

The main points being made in this first section are of a general rather than a specific nature. Firstly, without necessarily agreeing or disagreeing with the precise formulations of Kelley in terms of consensus, consistency and distinctiveness, we can abstract the central point that explanations of behaviour stem from knowledge and/or observations of social aspects of a situation; rather than from any direct access to causal factors *per se*. In a sense, this is the original insight provided by the work of Michotte, who showed that people would perceive patterns of causality where there were none.

Secondly, that making a particular type of attribution about a given situation tends to imply certain types of socially-evaluative (e.g. guilt/innocence; deserving/not deserving) verdicts about those involved. It is suggested that in areas where culturally established norms of right-and-wrong, or good-and-evil, exist, this tendency to produce an attributional verdict will be most marked; 'addiction' being one such area.

An Attributional Framework for Addiction

Earlier in this text, the 'Tom Hits Mary' contingency table was described, in order to make the point that explanations are derived from observations and beliefs about the nature of events, which predispose to certain modes of explaining. To that extent, explanation is a type of inference rather than an objective report on the causal nature of the universe.

To illustrate the point in a more directly pertinent way, we may draw up a similar, speculative, table describing the observations that might lead to explanation in terms of 'addiction.' It must be emphasised that this example is not data based, and as it stands it creates a number of problems; but it might at least serve as a stimulus to the reader to find the flaws in the argument and construct a better model for themselves.

It is suggested, subject to the above provisos, that explanation in terms of addiction has, like Kelley's example, three basic properties. These are:

i) a person is felt by him/herself and by others to carry out some behaviour too often, whilst neglecting other perceived moral responsibilities.
ii) the specific behaviour in question is seen by the larger society as shameful or morally reprehensible.
iii) the behaviour itself has an impact on the individual involved, but has no *direct* impact on others.

The interesting thing about these suggestions is that, with a certain amount of squeezing, they will fit into Kelley's system if a little imperfectly. For example, statement i) concerning behaviours that are perceived as occurring 'too much' resembles Kelley's consistency dimension. Statement ii) clearly has something to do with Kelley's consensus dimension; in terms of which drug use is low, since most people do not use drugs. This situation is supported by a moral consensus (in this case, high) that drug use is 'bad'. Finally, in terms of statement iii) the object of drug-using behaviour is the user him/herself, which can be seen as highly distinctive using Kelley's terminology.

Using this system, then, it is possible to translate the three attributional characteristics of addiction roughly into Kelley's framework, and we can then use these statements to play the same kinds of games that we played with the Tom-hits-Mary matrix. For example, whilst compliance with all three requirements leads to the attribution of addiction, endorsement of numbers i) and ii) only (i.e. the behaviour is seen as occurring too much; and the behaviour is seen as morally bad; but it *does* affect other people directly) leads to the attribution 'crime' rather than the attribution 'addiction'. This is reflected in the clear distinction between 'using' and 'pushing' drugs in terms of sentencing policy.

In a similar way, we might argue that behaviour consistent with statements i) and iii) (it happens too much; it is *not* seen as bad; it does not affect other people) leads to the attribution 'eccentric'; whilst i) alone (it happens too much; it is not bad; but it *does* affect other people) might be taken to imply commitment or dedication to a cause.

Not all combinations make obvious sense, however, and the reader is invited to make his/her own improvements to the suggested system. Nonetheless, the aim here is merely to attempt to demonstrate that the somewhat bland 'Tom Hits Mary' example can, with a little surgery, be made to apply in more complex and dynamic contexts, including drug use.

It needs to be reiterated that Kelley's model is only one of many approaches to 'explaining the act of explanation,' and that other frameworks sometimes prove more constructive in the area of addiction and drug misuse. As we shall see later, whilst Kelley's constructs appear to have some face validity, actual empirical evidence suggests that a different attributional framework fits the addiction data better; in particular, an interaction between the two dimensions *locus* and *stability* is best supported by the research literature, and appears to have the best attributional utility.

Addiction: A Stable/Internal Attribution

The pioneering work on the application of attribution theory to the description of addiction was carried out in several studies, mainly of smokers, in the late 70s and 80s. The work of Eiser must rank high on any list of important influences with respect to this development, and reference to specific pieces of research will be made in the chapter that follows. In a number of theoretically important studies, Eiser showed that a majority of smokers saw themselves as 'addicted'. This 'addicted' group of smokers were also in a 'dissonant state,' insofar as they were aware of, and afraid of, the consequences of smoking for their personal health. Eiser suggested that the 'addiction' explanation served as a means of lessening this dissonance, since by defining themselves as addicted the smokers implied that their smoking behaviour was outwith their personal volitional control. Therefore, dissonance was reduced by the cognition that although the habit was harmful, it was neither 'their fault' nor within their capacity to behave differently. Furthermore, in a 1982 paper, there was an indication that stable attributions for smoking were associated with failure to stop. In this context, a stable attribution is one which explains some behaviour in terms of factors which are unlikely to change.

Earlier in the text, the dimension of internal-external was discussed, the poles of the dimension being exemplified by explanations in terms of dispositional factors (internal) or situational (external) factors. We have now introduced a second specifically Weiner-type dimension, namely that of *stability*, which was also described in an earlier chapter. Eiser pinpointed these two dimensions (locus × stability) as being of primary importance in the context of addiction research, with addiction being defined by a particular interaction between the two.

The stable/unstable dimension underlies an attribution insofar as it 'explains' behaviour in terms of factors which range from enduring to transient. We have argued, for example, that poor examination performance explained in terms of lack of ability implies a stable state of affairs. The implication is that if the candidate tries again at a later date, he/she is going to fail once more, and to keep failing. On the other hand, if the explanation is that the candidate had a bad cold, the implication is that better performance might result at a later data when the cold has cleared up; the attribution is thus unstable.

Note however that both intelligence and a bad-cold are *internal* explanations, even though the implications for future examination success are quite different. One can envisage the reciprocal of the above, where two stable attributions have quite different implications by virtue of being either internal or external (e.g. disease conceptualised as either genetic in origin, or as a response to some environmental constant). The point being made in this dicussion of locus and stability attributions is that the implications of a given form of explanation derive from the interaction of the two, rather than being uniquely determined by either. For example, explaining poor examination performance in terms of a cold makes use of the unstable-internal ends of the two dimensions, since a cold is a property of the person that is temporary. On the other hand, if we attribute failure to 'being unlucky with the questions that came up', we are still using the unstable end of the dimension (i.e. next time we might be luckier) but in conjunction with an external (situational) locus. In either case, we can hope for success next time, even though the meanings of that success might be rather different. On the other hand, lack of ability is a stable internal attribution; prejudice on the part of the examiner is also stable but external. In either case we can anticipate failure on future occasions, although once again the meaning of that failure might be different. Ideally, therefore, prediction requires more than just one of these dimensions; it requires to take into account interactions of the two which produce common outcomes, each with a particular significance. Thus, whilst both external × stable and internal × stable imply continuing drug use, one implies 'helpless victim of circumstances', whilst the other implies 'helpless victim of disease'.

In attributional terms, 'addiction' represents just such a combination of *stable* and *internal* attributions. This form of explanation can legitimise drug-related behaviours insofar as it places them, in a sense, where the person cannot 'get at them' and thereby removes the element of volition; and hence absolves any 'guilty verdict' that might otherwise attach to the behaviour. It also implies that radical changes to enduring environmental conditions, such as might be suggested by a stable × external combination, will not do the trick either. No other combination captures these essential features of 'addiction'; that is, no personal responsibility and no hope of change.

Finally, it is worth re-stating that the attribution literature suggests that, in the absence of anything else, an internal locus generally implies personal responsibility, whereas an external locus suggests that events are outwith the actors hands. However, we have seen that in conjunction with stability, an internal attribution can come to serve the function usually served by an external attribution. The insight provided by Eiser was in fact that addiction was an internal attribution which, by virtue of being paired with stability, operated very much like an external attribution.

Attributional Bias

It now becomes necessary to discuss the implications of the attributional approach, in the light of evidence showing how people often introduce systematic bias into the attributions they make, and how the nature of the bias varies according to circumstances. The importance of this exciting fact is that it reveals that people have an intuitive grasp of the principles of attribution theory, and make use of it in their everyday lives. Since explanation derives from the way events are perceived, *people can lead others to make causal inferences about their behaviour by describing events and situations in particular ways. Furthermore, by explaining good or bad acts in terms of dispositional or situational factors, they can influence the kinds of verdicts that people arrive at with respect to their behaviour.* This intuitive, almost second-nature grasp of attributional principles is the key to its everyday functionality; and the fact that such functionality exists is illustrated by the extensive literature on attributional bias.

The reader should bear in mind the simple point being made. Namely, because different types of explanations are sometimes (as with drugs) associated with moral evaluations, there is often a clear advantage in one type of explanation rather than another, since this determines the moral inferences and verdicts that an audience will see as appropriate. In fact, the research literature shows that there are identifiable sources of bias in the explanations people offer; and the functionality of the biases may be revealed by examining the circumstances in which they occur.

The fact that the functional nature of attribution is understood and employed at an everyday level is illustrated by a non-research-based example concerning a tragic climbing accident on the mountain K2, the second-highest peak in the world. During the 1986 Himalayan season thirteen people died attempting to climb the mountain by various routes. A number of teams succeeded in reaching the summit, but lost members on the way down; amongst these being the mountaineer Kurt Diemberger and his climbing companion Julie Tullis. Almost after all hope had been abandoned for the pair, Diemberger was discovered in an exhausted state, having made a miraculous escape from the mountain in appalling conditions. Julie Tullis, his climbing partner, was dead however.

Later, Diemberger gave an explanation for what had happened; an explanation which was heard and subsequently reported by the climbing writer Jim Curran (Curran 1989). Curran commences with the comment that there appears to be 'a tendency for climbers (particularly in the upper echelons) to take a rather schizophrenic view of their abilites', this comment deriving primarily from Curran's own astute observations of the types of explanations that top climbers frequently offer for their successes and failures. According to Curran, Diemberger explained his own situation in the following words:

> 'We climbed our mountain of mountains. Destiny took Julie away'

Commenting on this explanation, Curran writes (page 174):

> 'Is this a coded way of saying, 'Through our skill, experience and determination we succeeded, but then we had some bad luck that we could do nothing about?' This is a mountaineering parallel to the motorist's defence, 'I was just driving along minding my own business when this car pulled out in front.' In other words, there is a strong temptation to give yourself the credit when everything is going well, but blame fate, the weather or other people when it isn't.'

Curran's observations imply that the explanations given by top climbers derive primarily from the nature of the consequences of their own behaviour, and by implication shed very little light on actual conditions on the mountain. The analogy between Curran's observations about mountaineers explanations and the present arguments about drug users explanations, is clear. The process whereby the explanation offered is configured so as to meet the psychological needs of the explainer is common to both. Consequently, such explanations shed more light on the explainer than on mountains or drugs.

The Actor-Observer Effect

Classic work in the area of attribution was carried out by Jones and Nisbett (1971), who investigated the differences in the ways people explained a) their own and b) other people's behaviour. One of their best-known findings in the area of 'actor-observer' differences was a tendency for 'actors (i.e. people explaining their own behaviour – author) to attribute their actions to situational requirements, whereas observers (i.e. people explaining other people's behaviour – author) tend to attribute the same actions to stable personal dispositions'.

In simple terms, this finding suggests that we tend to explain our own behaviour in terms of circumstances and situations to which we have to respond; whereas we explain other people's behaviour in terms of characteristics and properties of that person. Since this principle emerges from studies which for the most part have concerned neutral or positive behaviours, the bias is primarily 'self-effacing', rather like the magnanimous winner attributing his/her own success to chance factors, and other's success to ability. The pay-off is that possible future social interactions are eased; one is seen as Mr.Nice Guy.

Although several other important pieces of research have supported the notion of actor-observer differences as outlined above, it should be clear that it does not represent a general theory of social attribution. Even without the support of the subsequent research literature, one quickly realises that it is unlikely that people will attribute their own actions to circumstances and other people's behaviour to dispositional factors in all situations. The effect therefore may be strategic, and possibly disingenuous. For example, a self-performed 'good' act explained in terms of circumstances will present as appropriate modesty in some situations; but it may also rob the actor of worth and credit, since all semblance of personal ability or intention is removed unless there is obvious contrary evidence (e.g. one has just won Wimbledon).

In a complementary fashion, a 'bad' act explained in terms of personal factors implies volition and hence blame, whereas the circumstantial explanation implies that the fault lies with the situation rather than with the actor. If our contention of 'functional attribution' is to be sustained, therefore, the general principle implied by the actor-observer effect ought to be very much modified when the labels 'good' or 'bad' are applied to the behaviour in question. Specifically, the explanation ought to be modified by the extent to which it implies credit on the one hand, or blame on the other.

Self-Serving Bias

In fact, the above intuitions are supported by research which shows that the kinds of explanations offered for our own behaviour are modified when issues like blame and credit are involved. Specifically, it appears that people tend to attribute their own behaviour to internal (dispositional) factors when behaviour has a positive outcome, and to external (situational) factors when it has a negative outcome (e.g. Miller and Ross 1975; Bradley 1978; Weary 1980). This type of bias is known as 'self-serving.' The fact that attributions change when positive as opposed to negative issues are involved supports the contention that people can and do explain their behaviour in a primarily functional manner when the situation requires it, with the aim of controlling the verdicts that will be made by others.

There is another form of bias which is not normally conceptualised as self-serving, but which nonetheless has a clear self-serving component, and which consequently warrants inclusion here. It is a type of actor observer effect of an opposite and somewhat less-than-charitable nature, namely the tendency to attribute good acts by others to situational factors, whilst acts with negative outcomes are attributed to dispositional factors. For example, in a study of student teachers carried out by Johnson, Feigenbaum and Weiby (1964), it was found that when explaining success amongst their pupils, the teachers made reference to their own teaching. However, when asked to explain pupil failure, the teachers referred to characteristics of the pupil. The uncharitable or 'unacceptable face' of attribution has also revealed itself in studies of explanations for girls success at school in subjects which are technological or traditionally male-dominated. In such a setting, male success is likely to be attributed to natural ability, whilst the girls are more usually credited with hard work. Even more depressingly, the girls are more likely to devalue their own performance by explaining their examination success in terms of being lucky with the questions, rather than ability in the subject. The implications of such findings have been discussed elsewhere (Lochel 1983).

This darker side of the attributions people make has been less extensively researched, and to some extent remains relatively neglected. For example, the literature suggests a general tendency to explain other's success in terms of dispositional factors, whilst failure is explained in terms of circumstances; findings which probably reflect social-class limitations to the range of contexts in which attributions have been investigated rather than anything else. Specifically, such a rule applies only in social contexts where there is a desire to praise and encourage those who succeed; and a complementary desire to ease the pain of failure. But whilst such findings may hold true in a given type of social milieu, there also exist family and sub-cultural norms according to which achievement is treated with scorn and externally attributed ('Oh yes. He's got a degree now. He comes back here after three years at the University and he thinks he knows it all. Of course, he would never have got there if it hadn't been for us. . . . .') and failure is attributed to internal factors ('You never were any good at this, and you never will be, sunshine. You just haven't got what it takes.'). Clearly, self-serving bias can have many faces, only one of which has been fully explored. The origins, implications and consequences of such 'credit-removing/blaming' patterns merit more detailed exploration than the more commonly studied 'praising/excusing' patterns, and it is reassuring therefore to find the recent literature tempered by studies of the 'unacceptable face' of attribution from time to time.

Positivity Bias

The final type of bias to be mentioned here is general positivity bias, and it's inclusion stems partly from the comments made immediately above. It is a form of bias which apparently shows all concerned in a very favourable and sanguine light. 'Positivity bias' is said to occur when people's explanations for their own behaviour are extended to cover the behaviour of others; that is, the reasons for our own actions are the ones given to explain other people's actions also. Normally, this refers to a tendency to explain our own good actions in terms of dispositional or internal causes, and our bad actions in terms of circumstances; a set of principles which is then also employed when we are subsequently asked to account for someone else's behaviour (Feather and Simon 1971; Freize and Weiner 1971; van der Pligt and Eiser 1983). The principle underlying positivity bias thus looks vaguely altruistic on the surface.

However, it is possible to imagine an inverse form of positivity bias, which would probably have to be termed 'negativity' bias, when forms of explanation are preferred which remove credit and maximise blame for our own behaviour, and this account is extended to others. For example, in a study by Coggans and Davies (1988 *op cit*) to be discussed later, drug users extended certain explanations for their own drug use to others. This was not so much positivity bias, as the drug users implying 'I know it's bad, but everyone else is just as bad as I am.' In other words, a *self-serving* positivity bias whose function was to lessen perceived culpability by implying low distinctiveness.

Some Thoughts on the Possibility of Paradoxical Attribution

Three types of well-researched bias have been briefly described above, and the interested reader should pursue this extensive line of enquiry through the references provided. However, in each case an attempt was made to suggest that the accounts are in some sense incomplete; that there is something missing. In particular, there is a suspicion that the real meaning of an attributional bias (that is, its function) requires a closer examination of the context in which it is made. Simply saying that a self-serving bias or a positivity bias is revealed, does not in itself give an adequate understanding of a particular attribution. We have already shown, for example, how a positivity bias may be either altruistic in the sense of extending one's own positive motives to include others; or self-serving in the sense of extending one's negative motives to others. It's meaning cannot thus be fully understood without reference to the context in which it is made.

A similar point has been made by Newcombe and Rutter, in two critical papers (Newcombe and Rutter, 1982a; 1982b), in which it is argued that certain existing frameworks for the analysis of attributions (principally Kelley's ANOVA model) do not reveal their social meanings insofar as context is more or less excluded from the analysis. Newcombe and Rutter basically see the Kelley ANOVA model as an attempt to impose a static quasi-statistical model of inference-making on material that is inappropriately dynamic in nature, and interactive at a level that goes far beyond Kelley's propositions. The point is strongly made that the surface content of an attribution may frequently give little guide to its meaning within a dynamic interaction.

Returning to the suggestion that attributions are not merely ways of arriving at explanations, but that they serve functions for the person doing the explaining, we may consider more closely what those functions are whilst trying to take into account how specific contextual effects may influence the process. High on any list of functions comes self-presentation, and in a general sense all other functions may be subsumed under this label. However, regardless of whether the person is seeking to maximise credit, minimise blame, increase personal control or preserve self-esteem, the act of explaining will take place in a given social setting, and the explanation will be offered to another person who will in turn arrive at conclusions about the speaker on the basis of what he or she hears. Consequently, the explanation offered will also embody certain assumptions, made on the basis of limited information, by the speaker about the listener, and about his/her likely reactions to what is said within the circumstances prevailing. The functionality of the explanation will thus derive from these contextual factors; it is not inherent in the words themselves.

Now let us return to a consideration of a paper mentioned earlier (Davies and Baker *op cit*) in which two contrasting interviewers received markedly different reports from the same sample of heroin users. As part of that study, the heroin users responded to a small number of attributional-type questions. It will be recalled that to the 'straight' interviewer subjects presented themselves as more addicted, whereas to the drug-wise interviewer they gave the impression of having more choice and greater control. Now, given our assumption that self-presentation would be a central, and common, feature in both interviews, we have to ponder the question as to why subjects gave significantly different answers on the two occasions. That is, why should the explanation change if self-presentation is a main, and common function on both occasions?

Clearly, the change only makes sense as a response to differing interviewer characteristics, assumptions about what those differing characteristics imply, and an attempt to ensure that favourable 'verdicts' will be made by the interviewers in the different circumstances pertaining. Self-presentation is still the motivating factor, but it is important to realise that this works *not* through a fixed type of surface verbal script, but at the level of a social/ linguistic deep structure. That is, through the ability to present oneself appropriately in different contexts so that different people will in turn make the required type of attribution despite contextual variability. Consequently, the function of an attribution cannot be discerned simply from its semantics; elucidation of function requires that context be taken into account.

The idea of man as 'naive scientist', or as 'naive lawyer' thus needs some further elaboration, since it is apparent that the attributions people make serve the function of eliciting, in turn, desired verdicts from others. This implies the ability to predict how other people will react to a particular explanation, and to provide a type of account that will elicit a favourable response in different contexts. In such situations people are not so much naive scientists or lawyers, or indeed naive anything, so much as experts to varying degrees in the management and control of attributions. In other words, people are able to construct their explanations on the basis of their knowledge and experience of the *attributions that others are likely to make about them*; and when this occurs, attribution may be said to have a strategic component.

It is worth pointing out, in passing, that these conclusions arrived at on the basis of studies of attribution have also been arrived at by social theorists, by way of a very different route involving sociological theory and the exploration of the inadequacies of Left Realism. For example, Mugford and O'Malley (1990) write:

> 'Vocabularies of motive for actions, especially socially pro-
> scribed actions, are complex. It is not simply that they are 'false'
> in the sense that those who offer them seek to mislead. Rather,
> what constitutes a warrantable account at any one time and
> place, warrantable both to others *and to the person offering the
> account*, is subject to change according to context or setting.
> Thus the experience of users, and of their working class kin,
> friends, victims, neighbours and so on cannot be used to
> construct an explanation of action nor to form a generalised
> social policy concerning drugs and drug use.'

At this point, the argument becomes much more straightforward. Firstly we may say that any satisfactory general theory of attribution has to go beyond the specific semantic content of attributions, since the same attributional explanation can serve different functions in different circumstances; and the same functions can be served by different explanations, again according to circumstance. Secondly, people have an intuitive understanding of how attributions operate, without which they would be unable to use attribution as a functional social tool in the ways that they do.

From this basis, it is simple step to postulate the notion of 'paradoxical attribution', that is, a type of attribution in which the surface semantic features imply something opposite to the function that is actually being served. Unfortunately, paradoxical attribution *per se* has no research history, and indeed would require a revised methodological approach. Clearly, if the idea of paradoxical attribution has any merit, almost any attribution can be interpreted as supporting any given position *ex post facto*, a point raised in the Coggans and Davies (*op cit*) paper unless context is taken into account. Consequently, there has to be a methodology based on *prediction within context*, to replace the standard model which investigates attributions in a contextual vacuum; that is, as though the participants brought nothing to the transaction apart from some information about consistency, consensus and distinctiveness (or whatever attributional dimensions) relating only to the specific act in question. This is a theoretical deficiency and indicates a possible direction in which future research might proceed.

The papers by Newcombe and Rutter (*op cit*) reveal a similar line of thinking. Newcombe and Rutter (1982b) cite two examples from Ross (1977) to illustrate the idea of semantic ambiguity, which is the first step towards the idea of paradoxical attribution. Ross provides two statements which are equivalent in meaning but opposite in terms of an internal-external dimension, as follows:

> *'Jack bought the house because it was secluded.'*
> *'Jack bought the house because he wanted seclusion.'*

The two statements, according to Newcombe and Rutter, are 'conceptually identical' (p. 99). Attributions to internal and/or external causes would, the author argues, be 'trivially true and totally uninformative' since the meaning of the sentence in some sense transcends this level of analysis.

Newcombe and Rutter's argument is correct so far as it goes; but to ·some extent they themselves ignore the central feature of the argument, namely context. In the absence of any knowledge of context, the categorisation of the statements as internal or external is indeed trivial. However, provision of strong contextual cues and internal motives can make it highly functional to prefer one mode of presentation to the other. For example, suppose we know that Jack bought the house on behalf of an elderly relative. In that context, stating that he bought it because it was secluded leads the listener to infer that Jack was aware of the fact that the elderly relative liked seclusion. On the other hand, a statement to the effect that Jack bought it because he himself liked seclusion implies that it was purchased to meet his own personal requirements rather than the elderly relative's. Finally, knowledge that Jack *in fact* likes seclusion reveals the first form of presentation ('Jack bought the house because it was secluded') to be primarily functional for Jack (it disguises his true motives) in a way that the second form does not. In other words knowledge of context is the key factor that makes a functional interpretation, and a sensible differentiation between the statements, possible. Consequently, whilst Newcombe and Rutter argue quite correctly against the Kelley notion that meaning emerges 'automatically' from the semantics of consensus/consistency/distinctiveness and their interactions, it does not follow that the choice of internal or external locus is thereby demonstrated to be of no significance. In the 'Jack bought the house. . .' example, the locus dimension is only trivial and uninformative when this is also treated in a contextual vacuum. In the absence of context, attributions can mean all things to all men, as noted in the Coggans and Davies paper (*op cit*); but provision of a context makes their functions clear, and their interpretation possible.

However, returning to the idea of paradoxical attribution, we require to find examples where the semantics of what is said actually represent the *opposite* of what is meant at a deeper level; not merely examples where choice of locus appears to make no difference, as suggested by Newcombe and Rutter. In fact, it is not difficult to find examples which appear to fit the bill, with some of the most obvious examples coming from the realm of sport. For example, a cyclist in the Tour de France won the Polka-Dot jersey after a stunning effort during which he laboured for some eight hours over 150 miles of alpine climbs, and then explained his victory by saying 'I just happened to be in the right place at the right time'. On the surface, this is a *situational* attribution, but it actually conveys the meaning 'extreme modesty', which is a *dispositional* characteristic. Paradoxically, given existing beliefs about correct comportment at moments of triumph, the *only* way to ensure that the audience would make a favourable dispositional judgement was to provide a situational explanation, no matter how unlikely the latter may seem. It remains only to say that a number of people of genius, such as the Scottish cyclist Robert Millar, have been judged 'inept' in their dealings with the press on the basis of their inability (i.e. unwillingness) to make functional attributions of the 'socially skilled' type; that is, the failure to answer obvious questions with the obvious, socially functional, answer.

The notion of the 'good loser' and the 'magnanimous winner' are well-known examples of paradoxical attribution which sometimes reach absurd heights. The winner gains extra positive dispositional regard by making his victory seem a matter of chance or circumstance; the loser achieves the same thing by making dispositional attributions about the victor.

Within this morass of highly functional paradoxical attributions it is refreshing therefore to find 'socially unskilled' heroes, like Eric Bristow the darts player, who when invited by a sports commentator to make the mandatory self-effacing comments about how he won a darts championship declined the offer, instead choosing words to the effect that basically no-body else was half as good as he was, and that he could beat the opposition blindfolded.

Belief in God: A Functional, External, Paradoxical Locus

Returning now to the central theme of addiction, it is apparent that the notion of paradoxical attribution has profound implications for one of the the most influential of traditional treatment approaches. We have noted in previous chapters how AA and other similar agencies encourage their clients to believe that they are powerless to control their own behaviour, and that they must therefore recruit the power of some higher being to assist them; that is, God in some form. Paradoxically, by believing that the power of a higher being.is the only thing that can help them in their helplessness, they cease to be helpless, because belief in an *external* higher power changes *internal* motivation. *By invoking an all-powerful external locus for the control of their behaviour, they increase their internal desire to behave differently.* A paradoxical external locus in fact has the most profound internal implications.

From such a viewpoint, it is clear why the success of this approach is critically dependent of the capacity of the individual to invoke and believe in a higher power. With respect to problems of addiction, *believing in God (in some form) and believing in the medical model (in some form) are similar insofar as they both involve an external locus. However, belief in God has a paradoxical effect on personal motivation that the medical model, unaided, lacks. That is why belief in God or some higher power is so often involved in 'recovery'.* It remains only to add that, once the principles are understood, the same results should be achievable without recourse to either God or the medical model.

The Third Stream

There is a need for a *third stream* in dealing with the problems of substance use. This is a stream which invokes neither God nor the medical model, but relies on natural processes of attribution and paradoxical attribution to return control to the individual concerned without recourse to either a) scientism or b) superstition.

10
Functional Explanations for Drug Use

The idea of functional explanation is by no means new. For example, similar arguments have been put forward with respect to the issue of 'impression management' elsewhere within the general social psychology literature. Whilst impression management tends to have more-or-less explicit cognitive and strategic connotations of a type that are not implied within the present argument, the idea that verbal reports serve functions which are defined by context is common to both. However, the impact of this type of thinking upon research in the addictions has been very limited, especially with regard to the possibility of functional or strategic explanations for drug use.

In a previous chapter, reference was made to the work of Eiser, whose application of attributional theory to studies of smoking behaviour has been fundamental to the development of the current line of thinking. The time has now come to examine in more detail this ground-breaking work, and a selection of related work by others who have sought to extend the application of attribution theory to the problems of substance use and misuse. Since the first edition of this book the area has become livelier and the reader should be aware that the work has now expanded both in terms of the number of publications, and in terms of breadth of reference; for example, there are aspects of the work of Prochaska and DiClementi *et al* (e.g. 1988, 1991), and especially of Bandura (1986) which may now be construed as loosely attributional in nature; or at least, as having some bearing on the notion of addiction-as-attribution. The most recent theoretical developments in the debate are reviewed in a related text (Davies 1997) though brief mention of additional work is given towards the end of this chapter.

J. Richard Eiser (1977 et seq)

Overall, Eiser's contribution represents the most coherent body of work on the attribution of addiction. However, Eiser is not solely an addiction researcher, but an attribution theorist and social psychologist at a much broader level, with a prolific output on many aspects of cognitive social psychology. Despite a period at the Addiction Research Unit, part of the Institute of Psychiatry in London, his work is probably better known to social psychologists than to addiction workers, and his appearances at addiction conferences are fairly infrequent. His contribution illustrates the value of the relatively detached view which can sometimes bring fresh theoretical perspectives into areas which otherwise may become moribund. And research into substance misuse has become exactly that; theoretically moribund.

Eiser's most important contribution to the addiction literature emerged from a number of investigations of the reasons that smokers gave for smoking. Their reasons related in various ways to their beliefs about cancer and the dangers of smoking, and to their perceptions as to how difficult it would be to attempt to stop. From these early studies emerged the conclusion that explanations in the area of addiction made the most sense when viewed within the theoretical context of attribution theory. Eiser's work has a distinctive style to it. It is clearly social psychological in nature, makes no concessions at all to clinical impression, and uses measurement scales which are extremely concise. Thus, whilst a clinical study might involve collecting 150 data points from semi-structured in-depth interviews with individual clients attending a clinic or treatment centre, Eiser's early work typically might involve samples of sixth-formers in school, or groups of the normal population obtained perhaps through an appeal on television, and a short self-completion questionnaire within which the actual attribution component might be pared down to no more than four or five items. From such studies emerges a far-reaching conclusion, which nonetheless goes largely disregarded. Whilst clinicians still catalogue the stated reasons given by drug users for their relapses and remissions on the assumption that these are statements about causality, and the press and media invariably resort to junkies when they want to know what drug use in really like, Eiser has written (1986 *op cit*):

> 'What people say about their smoking reflects much the same learning process as is involved in the acquisition of the habit itself.'

The importance of this comment resides in the fact that it sees an 'addicted behaviour' (in this case, smoking), and acceptable ways of explaining that behaviour, as emerging from a common learning process. By contrast, many addiction workers still assume that these are independent, and therefore that one can discover the causes of drug use simply by asking people to say what they are.

The work referred to took place in the middle and late 1970's, when some seven or eight papers were published, mostly on the topic of attribution theory and its relevance to smoking. Given the number of papers and their implications, it is ironic that whilst academics with an interest in social cognition can usually be expected to know about Eiser's work with smokers, a majority of those working in a practical sense with addiction problems are probably unaware of this important contribution. This failure of theory to impinge on practice is, however, a general problem. Five papers published in the 70's formed the basis for Eiser's subsequent conclusions. All concerned smokers' attributions about aspects of the habit, both in themselves and amongst other people, and there was a theoretical concern with actor/observer effects. Of these papers (Eiser *et al* 1977a, 1977b, 1978a, 1978b and 1978c) the one by Eiser, Sutton and Wober (1977a *op cit*) seems to have laid the foundations. In this piece of work Eiser and his colleagues obtained the co-operation of the Independent Broadcasting Association, who were distributing programme appreciation diaries to a representative sample of some 1790 viewers in the North West of England. Attached to these diaries was a brief questionnaire about smoking and attributions compiled by the Eiser team. A programme about smoking was broadcast on January 22nd, 1976 and the diary work took place during the week beginning January 19th. The method produced a diary-return rate of 25.2 percent, which included 368 completed smoking questionnaires. The smoking questionnaire was pared down to a minimum, with the relevant content consisting of three questions about smoking behaviour, four attributional questions for smokers, four attributional questions *about* smokers for non-smokers, and perhaps one or two additional bits and pieces not apparent from the text of the article. The subjects were classified as smokers, ex-smokers and never smokers, and the data for the most part were scored in terms of simple three-point scales. The single most salient finding from the study was that seeing smoking as an 'addiction' was mainly a function of whether the respondent smoked or not. In addition, heavier smokers and those who obtained the most pleasure from cigarettes were distanced from other smokers by the attribution of addiction to themselves. Also, smokers not attempting to give up the habit were differentiated from those who claimed to have made the attempt, again in terms of the self-attribution of addiction.

Eiser's conclusions with respect to health education are as follows:

> '. . .account must be somehow taken of the pleasure smokers derive from smoking itself and of the prime important of this factor in maintaining their behaviour, in spite of warnings of dangers to health. Secondly, associating the concept of addiction with cigarette smoking, whatever deterrent effects this may have for the would-be smoker, may well make the existing smoker feel less able to give up. . .'

Eiser thus implies that people smoke because they like it, but that this motive is given insufficient credence; and that associating the addiction concept with smoking makes it harder for smokers to stop. Applied to drug use at a general level, these two statements provide a fair summary of the message underlying this book.

As is invariably the case with Eiser's work, there is a conscious attempt to extend existing theory, at a time when some addiction workers have adopted an increasingly anti-theoretical stance, believing instead that immediate action is required no matter if such action is based on nothing more than received wisdom. Since the early days, Eiser has developed the range, subject matter, and types of methodology employed, so this body of work now includes studies of users of illicit drugs, and various forms of multivariate analysis. Maintaining the theoretical perspective throughout Eiser has shed light on self-serving bias and positivity bias (see Van der Pligt and Eiser *op cit*) and has also produced evidence that the attributional styles of in-patients and out-patients at drug clinics might be capable of differentiation, and possibly have some clinical value.

One specific contribution to the literature deserves mention, namely the 'sick or hooked' distinction proposed by Eiser and Gossop (1979) which has entered into the general currency of addiction to some extent. The study in question involved an investigation of 'addict's' perceptions of their own drug dependence. The subjects were 40 (30 male, 10 female) outpatients who were individually administered a short questionnaire comprising 15 attitude items and 10 measures of locus of control. Although no clear picture emerged in terms of locus of control (an inconclusive finding which resembles similar 'locus' studies carried out on other groups) a factor analysis described two main components accounting for 31.5% of the total variance. These

were the 'hooked' and 'sick' factors. The hooked factor was characterised by feelings of being 'really addicted', fear of withdrawals, belief in
the user's inability to give up drugs and an unwillingness even to
attempt the task. The sick factor on the other hand implied that the user
saw the problem in broader terms. Rather than being simply a drug
problem, there were other aspects to it, including problems in other life
areas. According to this view, the user was sick but at the same time
recovery was possible with the help of doctors.

In a sense, it is a pity that this particular piece of work is perhaps the
best known, since the picture emerging from the factor analysis is less
than clear-cut in attributional terms. Whilst the distinction between
sick and hooked is of interest, the failure of a clear attributional picture
to emerge in terms of sick v not sick, or hooked v not-hooked creates
problems. In other words, because there are elements of 'sick' in
'hooked', and of 'hooked' in 'sick', the attributional implications are
less easy to see.

It is apparent however that Eiser sees very clearly the implications of
attribution for the understanding of addiction (see for example Eiser
et al 1982, 1985; and Gossop and Eiser 1982) but he remains rather care-
ful about suggesting that attributions and behaviour might be linked in
any simple way. In addition, he suggests that 'expectancy seems to be
the critical link between attributions and behaviour, but the concept
itself is treated as relatively unproblematic in much attributional
research. On the other hand, research on the psychology of prediction
suggests that people's calculations of the likelihood of future events are
open to numerous biases.' (1982 *op cit*).

Perhaps it is this diffidence which is partly responsible for the fact that
Eiser's work is not seen in its true perspective in the addiction field. Eiser
is so concerned with the interrelation of attribution with other aspects of
social cognition that the major implication (i.e. that addiction is a type of
functional explanation) is lost sight of. By seeking for validation by way
of prediction and expectancy, the waters are muddied somewhat. At the
end of the day, the phenomena we refer to as prediction and expectancy
are also, usually, verbal statements given in response to questions. As
such, they are open to as much bias as any other verbal behaviour, and
their postulation as i) variables which represent internal psychological
entities (e.g. like attitudes, beliefs, values, opinions and so forth) and ii)
variables which can reasonably be conceptualised as independent, add
increased complexity to the issue, rather than offering any simplification.
We sometimes tend to assume that people make attributions whenever
we ask attribution questions, and stop doing so when we move on to a

new set of questions. In fact, one line of argument suggests that people's attributional styles manifest themselves, if at all, spontaneously and in many ways. Consequently, expectancy and prediction might be themselves nothing more or less than self-serving second-order 'attributions' in a slightly different form, offered in response to a different form of questioning, but stemming from the same social/linguistic 'deep structure'. In a sense, therefore, the formalisms of attribution theory may be merely specific manifestations of an underlying process which imbues statements of many kinds with a common substrate of functionality. It may be that this suggestion would fall within Eiser's intended remit when he writes, 'what seems to be needed in this area is a more integrative approach to social cognition that deals both with the processes of explanation and with the processes of prediction.'

For these reasons, one might conclude that the potential usefulness of the attributional approach will be realised not by further studies in the classic attribution mould, nor by studies which relate attribution to other difficult-to-operationalise concepts, but by trying to find out in some predictive sense (future or concurrent) the extent to which a given behaviour can be predicted from particular patterns of functional attribution. It may also be necessary to move beyond existing attributional frameworks, by adopting a more open-ended view of how attributional-type processes might manifest themselves, and by taking the functionality of a variety of types of verbal behaviour as the common basis for the development of further testable theory. This implies the need for a way of dealing with functionality which is lawful and replicable, something which attributional theory might offer.

Eiser's work is fundamental in suggesting the link between attribution and addiction, and in delineating the properties of addiction in attributional terms. If, at the end of the day we conclude that he declined to grasp the nettle, we must also concede that it was he who, in the first instance, pointed out that the addiction garden needed weeding.

Davies and Baker (1988)

This study has been mentioned previously in connection with methodological problems. It is briefly raised again here for substantive reasons, because the questionnaire included attribution items dealing with internal and external reasons for using drugs. These scales were brief, consisting of three internal statements, and three external statements, about drug use. Subjects simply rated each statement in terms of a two point true/false (or in the parallel form, yes/no) dichotomy.

It will be recalled that in this study, twenty drug users were interviewed on two occasions by a 'straight' interviewer and by a known drug user. It was anticipated that subjects would be more defensive to the 'straight' man than to the user, reporting lower consumption and fewer serious consequences of the habit to the former. This is in line with the assumption that people tend to under-report their bad habits when asked about them by researchers. In line with this expectation, it was anticipated that subjects would be more likely to present themselves in terms of the 'addict' stereotype to the straight interviewer than to the known user, on the grounds that explanations minimising personal responsibility would be more functional when accounting for drug use to someone perceived as a member of 'the establishment'.

However, the expectations about consumption and extent of the habit were disconfirmed. The picture presented to the straight interviewer was substantially more extreme than that offered to the known drug user. On the other hand it was certainly the case that subjects presented themselves more internally when interviewed by the straight man; that is, as more 'addicted'. Out of the twenty subjects, four scored the same on the internal scale, whilst 15 of the remainder changed in the direction of greater agreement with the 'internal' items. In ordinary language, the results from the attribution items showed that subjects presented themselves as being in much the same situation to both interviewers (there was no significant shift in 'external' ratings) but presented *themselves* in a different way.

We expected the drug users to present themselves to the straight interviewer as 'not as bad as one might expect', but also as battling with something beyond their control. However, the picture that emerged gave primacy to cognitive consistency over pragmatics; greater internality was associated with higher reports of consumption, and the straight researcher received the benefit of both these shifts.

Coggans and Davies (1988)

This study was also briefly mentioned in the section on attributional biases, but it is now appropriate to consider the findings in a little more detail. In this study, data were collected from 15 heroin users in Glasgow, each user being interviewed on three separate occasions at three-monthly intervals, using the same set of questions on each occasion. The study focussed on two aspects of attribution, with items being derived or adapted from certain existing scales dealing with the dimensions of *locus* and *stability*. Using these two dimensions, subjects were asked to give reasons for:

1) staying off heroin
2) relapsing
3) for the occurrence of unpleasant (negative) events generally, and
4) for the occurrence of positive events generally.

They answered this set of questions both with reference to themselves, and with reference to others, thus providing data on a possible actor/observer difference. The questionnaire thus examined two attributional dimensions, by four types of event, by self-other, yielding 32 items with two items at each combination of conditions.

Aspects of explanation that were relatively stable in the longer term were revealed by a cluster analysis based on mean scores over the three interviews, for each subject. The clusters were refined by Alpha, the analysis producing five clusters all with Alpha in excess of 0.75. The results accord at various points with the general attribution theory literature, and it is not difficult to derive *ex post facto* explanations of the function that these types of explanation might serve. For example, the heroin users explained their own relapses in terms of positive events, whilst staying off was associated with negative events. However, they described other people's relapses and remissions in terms of the more popular wisdom, that relapse was associated with bad times and remission with good times. It appears that in terms of this cluster structure, explanation for others' drug-use behaviour accorded with the popular stereotype of drug use as a response to stress. However, they explained their own use in terms of their own good reasons. This looks very much like some sort of actor/observer effect, possibly involving self-serving bias.

Other aspects of the data showed positivity bias, that is, sharing of certain types of explanations with others. This appeared to have a paradoxical aspect, insofar as sharing certain negative features with others might in fact be self-serving. That is, it diffuses personal responsibility by implying 'Look. I'm no worse than the others'.

Finally, the study grouped the users into two categories, a 'chronic' group whose pattern of use was more consistent on a day to day basis; and a 'sporadic' group whose use pattern was most variable. The analysis controlled for actual amount consumed by means of partial regression, so that differences in actual amounts consumed between the groups would not affect the results. The constant (chronic) users blamed stable, internal factors for not being able to stay off (i.e. they explained themselves in terms of an 'addiction' stereotype) whilst the variable users blamed unstable, external factors (i.e. luck or chance) for their pattern of use. This suggests a link between type of use and the nature of the reasons given for that use. Clearly, someone using drugs seven days a week can hardly blame their behaviour on 'bad luck' which would have to occur on a daily basis; and similarly, a sporadic user who uses Monday and Tuesday but not Wednesday and Thursday can hardly claim be an addict.

Replication of studies of this type is needed for a variety of reasons. Firstly, the findings emerge from a small sample of subjects, and the stable attribution patterns had to be 'fished for' by means of cluster analysis and factor scoring. More direct methods of analysis (e.g. by the use of between-group significance tests) failed to come up with very much that was useful. To the extent that a small subject pool had to be dredged by cluster analysis, the results are suspect.

Secondly, one possible criticism of Eiser's work (that the scales he used were too sparse to really get to the heart of the matter) took on a different appearance in the light of these preliminary efforts. It was clear to us that a great deal of noise lurked in the data as a consequence of the 'in-depth' attribution questionnaire/interview used. It seems likely that there is a limit to the number of questions about locus, stability, self, others, relapse and remission that can be asked without the exercise starting to become slightly surreal. Certainly, the assumption that one can ask strings of attribution questions on the assumption that every answer the subject gives is an undiluted, independent 'attribution' is open to serious question. It seemed to us that after a while, the exercise started to become unreal in the same way that extended repertory-grid procedures start to become unreal. The procedural commonality is the seemingly endless repetition of the same questions, each time with respect to a marginally different object, which leads us to the conclusion that there has to be a more concise and socially real way of obtaining the data required to test a theory. Certainly, any problems associated with the very spare Eiser type approach cannot be overcome simply by asking a lot more questions.

It remains only to stress once more that the study is attributional in conception and interpretation. Consequently, the question of whether a subject's answers were true of false is not the topic at issue. What is illustrated is the consistency between forms of explanation and self-reports of drug use. Although the experiment provided subjects with no clues as to the nature of any categorisation that might take place in terms of consumption pattern, subjects still revealed a tendency to explain particular patterns of consumption in consistent ways; ways that primarily made attributional sense of the pattern of use described.

McAllister and Davies (1991)

In the Coggans and Davies (*op cit*) study, differences in attribution were found between chronic and sporadic users, but the relationships were not strong. However, in that study subjects were not classified as chronic or sporadic until after all the data had been collected; subjects could thus not have been aware of this classification at the time of their interviews. Furthermore, during data collection there were no clues to the fact that such a comparison was to take place. Consequently, the differences in attribution emerged in circumstances where cues to the purpose of the study were minimal, and consequently the type of explanation that would be optimally functional would be difficult for subjects to envisage; in other words the 'implicit theory' was not at all clear.

McAllister and Davies (1991) hypothesised that in circumstances where cues to functionality were maximised within the experimental procedure, attributional differences would emerge in a clearer and more predictable form. Accordingly, McAllister devised a test/retest study in which subjects offered attributions for their smoking before and after the nature of the study was made clear. She used a set of Weiner-type items covering eight possible combinations of locus, stability and controllability, and predicted that there would be directional shifts in the 'addicted' combination (internal/stable/uncontrollable) as a consequence of an experimental manipulation.

At the first interview, a group of 20 women smokers with a minimum of five years' smoking history were interviewed. They were administered a questionnaire by the experimenter, which assessed extent of smoking and attributions for smoking. The interview was carried out in an informal manner, with subject and experimenter seated at the corner of a table so that subjects could plainly see the schedule and the answers being recorded. After completion of all first-phase interviews, subjects were dichotomised into two groups on the basis of the self-reported consumption data, to yield a heavy-smoking group and a light-smoking group. Significance tests *post hoc* showed no differences between the groups identified in terms of sex, age, marital status, employment status, or agency through which they were contacted.

Between five and seven weeks later, all subjects were reinterviewed by the same experimenter. However, on this occasion, each page of the interview schedule bore the subject's classification in capital letters at the top i.e. LIGHT SMOKER or HEAVY SMOKER. The experimenter pointed this out to subjects, before proceeding. The questionnaire contained the same attribution items as at the first interview.

The results of the study are shown in Table 2 below. In Table 2, scores on the crucial internal/stable/uncontrollable (ISU) dimension are given inside the box.

Table 2 Mean Ratings of the Attributions

	ESU	IUU	ESU	IUC	EUC	*ISU	EUU	ISC
Light Smokers								
Interview 1	2.8	6.0	3.5	5.1	6.3	5.7	1.1	3.8
Interview 2	5.0	7.8	3.4	5.5	6.8	2.4	2.3	2.4
Heavy Smokers								
Interview 1	2.3	6.1	3.4	5.1	6.0	3.9	1.4	5.1
Interview 2	3.2	6.8	3.7	2.6	4.9	4.9	1.5	5.6

From the above, it can be seen that at the first interview, the mean ratings on the internal/stable/uncontrollable dimension for the two groups were such that the light smokers exceeded the heavy smokers, but this difference was not statistically significant. At the second interview, however, the position was reversed, with the heavy smokers now making increased use of the 'addicted' attribution style. This difference was statistically significant. Analysis of variance showed a significant interaction between interview and group membership of exactly the type hypothesised and the nature of this interaction is clearly revealed in Fig. 5.

On learning of their categorisation as either light or heavy smokers, subjects thus made predictable attributional shifts from the position adopted at the first interview. Light smokers shifted markedly away from the 'addicted' attributional style, whilst those in the heavy-smoking category went in the opposite direction, towards more 'addicted'. Subjects thus took into account what they thought the experimenter thought of them, when selecting the appropriate attribution.

The study shows once again that explanation is not primarily veridical, but variable according to context. Moreover, there are specific implications for the clinical setting which probably warrant closer scrutiny. Clinicians may sometimes infer 'addiction' from client's self

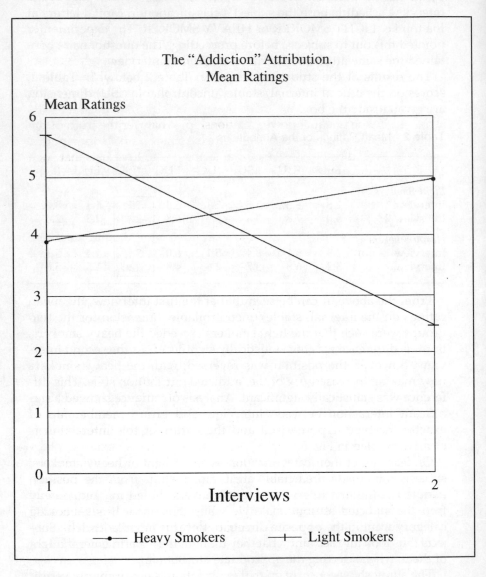

Fig. 5

reports and explanations for drug use, especially when such reports stress inability to control behaviour, overlooking the possibility that answers might be functional.

The effects found in this study are of particular interest since the style of interviewing here was informal and non-judgmental, so subjects should have felt less pressurised to explain their smoking in terms of factors that reduced personal responsibility. Within the clinical transaction, however, not only is the client aware that his/her responses are being evaluated, but the need to make functional shifts in attribution is increased by the unequal power relationship. Whatever the truth of the matter, the study implies that a closer examination of the therapeutic encounter would be of interest, insofar as the possibility exists that such transactions create their own 'script' deriving from the nature of the transaction itself.

In circumstances where someone presents at a clinic or agency with a drug problem, knowing that the therapist/counsellor also believes there is a problem, the idea that the attribution of 'addiction' might be an essential part of the script for *both* participants is intriguing. In game theory terms (see for example Hamburger 1979) it represents the Minimax point at which both participants agree simply because it is the best deal that can be struck for either individual, under the worst circumstances that the other can create.

Ogden and Wardle (1990)

In chapter 6 we addressed the problem of 'addictive' substances, and argued that despite the clear and differing pharmacological impact of different drugs on individual functioning, the essence of those behaviours we class as 'addicted' does not actually *require* an external pharmacology. Reference was also made to Orford's (*op cit*) text on excessive appetites, in which sexual and eating problems are subsumed under the same label as drug-based habits. Within this context, the work by Ogden and Wardle (1990) is of importance, firstly because it represents the most recent contribution by Wardle and her co-workers in the area of eating disorders, and specifically the problems of excessive and binge eating sometimes referred to as *bulimia nervosa*, which have received scant attention so far; and secondly because it reveals attributional shifts in the area of eating problems that are readily identifiable as the same as those found amongst people with drug problems, or substance-based 'addictions'.

The study is also of interest because it is partly attributional in a way that the classic studies of smokers by Eiser are not. One possible criticism of the earlier Eiser studies is that certain of the outcome variables are not particularly 'hard'. In the 1977 (*op cit*) study for example, attributions for addiction were related to self-reports from individuals about their ability or inability to attempt to stop smoking; specifically, those making 'addicted' types of attribution reported that they were unable to make the attempt to stop. It has been suggested by other workers that these early data would be stronger if the outcome criterion had been based on actual behaviour rather than statements about behaviour; a fundamental criticism which may however be applied to *any* type of research showing relationships between sets of verbal statements. To the extent that the criticism is valid, it applies to vast areas of research, and not just to Eiser's early studies.

In this instance, however, the criticism can be met. Eiser's later studies of drug users employ measures other than verbal reports, and the attributional aspects of the theory are thereby strengthened insofar as attributional links are established with actual drug-related behaviours. The Ogden and Wardle paper is important because it follows in this tradition, and further strengthens the attributional argument. Perhaps most important, it examines the link between an attribution measure taken at the start of the study, and subsequent behaviour: the classic attributional link.

Ogden and Wardle base their approach on the well-known text by Marlatt and Gordon (1985), and write as follows: 'The critical factor in the lapse/relapse process is hypothesised to be the way the individual attributes the causality of the original lapse. Marlatt and Gordon (1985) predict that if the individual attributes the cause to an internal cause, such as personal inadequacy or lack of self-control, the lapse is likely to become a full-blown relapse. However, if the original lapse is attributed to external events, such as social demands, the lapse remains a lapse, and restraint is restored.'

In the Ogden and Wardle study, 23 moderately-overweight women took part (a twenty-fourth subject did not complete the study). They were of mean age 37.6 years, weighed an average of 72.18 kg, and had an average Body Mass Index of 27.2. At the start of the study, the participants completed the Life Evaluation and Attribution Rating Scale (Brewin and Shapiro 1984) which looks at the extent to which subjects attribute negative and positive events to internal or external factors. All subjects attended a talk by a dietician and agreed to a diet which would restrict their calorie intake to 1,000kcal to 1,500kcal per day for six weeks. Subjects were interviewed weekly, and reported any dietary infringements that had taken place. Each subject was then instructed to recall one dietary infringement of special significance, and rate its causality on an amended form of the Attribution Style Questionnaire (Peterson *et al* 1982).

Scores on the Life Evaluation and Attribution Rating Scale showed that negative events were more frequently attributed internally by those who *subsequently* broke their diets; diet breaking and LEAR scores correlating 0.44 (p<.05). In addition, scores on the 'globality' dimension of the ASQ discriminated (p<.05) between those who relapsed fully and those who lapsed but regained control; though this finding does not support the attributional link since the measure was taken after the diet violation. Interestingly, Ogden and Wardle report less success with their other dimensions, though the paper fails to take into account the locus × stability interaction which is crucial to an understanding of the 'addiction' attribution.

Overall, the study shows that the attributional model of 'addiction' applies to excessive eating as well as to substance-based problems. Central is the finding that an internal style of attribution is associated with more frequent failures of dietary control; a key feature of addiction attributions. It is unfortunate that the authors do not explore the locus × stability interaction, however, since better discrimination appears to derive when this Eiser-type of interactive model is applied. On the other hand, the authors find that global attributions about the causes of a particular lapse are associated with more serious relapses; a finding which suggests new lines of theoretical development. In summary, Ogden and Wardle provide intriguing evidence suggesting that it is possible to discriminate between moderately-overweight women who break their diets, and those who do not, in terms of attributional measures. The most important finding relates to a measure of internal/external locus which was completed at the start of the study, and which predicted subsequent behaviour.

Hood (1988)

Hood's work derives from an unpublished Masters Thesis completed during 1987-88, which was highly regarded at the time. Unfortunately, Hood returned to Canada before the work could be written up for publication, and certain aspects of the methodology have subsequently proven unclear; it is to be regretted that she was unable to take this line of work to its proper conclusion. The work is briefly presented here as a contribution to the present debate, and as an indication of what might be possible, with the proviso that certain aspects of the data elicitation procedure are questionable.

Hood was interested in the development of the Health Belief Model (Becker *et al* 1977; Rosenstock 1966; 1974) proposed by King (1983 *op cit*). According to King, the predictive usefulness of the model is increased by the incorporation of attribution scales. Whilst King's work is of more general interest from the point of view of health, Hood was specifically interested in alcohol problems with special reference to women and the difficulties they encountered when seeking treatment. However, she also wanted to test certain of King's ideas about attribution theory and health in this slightly more specific context.

An important feature of Hood's work was a discriminant function analysis comparing problem-drinking and non-problem-drinking groups, performed with the aim of discovering which aspects of the data might potentially be of most use in a clinical or diagnostic setting. She was specially concerned to compare the Weiner and Kelley approaches to attribution measurement within the general Health Belief framework, and in so doing found a combination of attribution items which could predict membership of the problem-drinking/non-problem-drinking groups with considerable success. Two of the attribution items accounted for most of the variance explained (one Kelley and one Weiner-type item, namely consensus and effort) and these two alone could successfully assign subjects to the correct drinking group with 90% success overall.

The finding is of interest for two reasons. Firstly, the form of analysis chosen used attribution as the independent variable. That is, instead of starting with two criterion groups and asking to what extent their attributional styles differed as a function of group membership (the most usual approach) she tried to predict group membership on the basis of attributions. The approach is thus, in a weak sense, attributional. Secondly, the findings imply that successful discrimination between groups with and without drinking problems is possible without having recourse to questions seeking 'truth'; that is, without going through the highly context-dependent exercise of asking 'How much do you drink?' and similar consumption-type questions. In fact, in the present study the attribution items predicted group membership almost as well as the more extensive set of consumption questions, which predicted with 96% accuracy. However, in the absence of specific detail on certain procedural points, the study remains enigmatic.

Edwards, Brown, Duckitt, Oppenheimer, Sheehan and Taylor (1987)

There are a number of reasons for making particular mention of the study by Edwards *et al* (1987). The paper has a number of interesting features, not the least of which is that it comes from the Addiction Research Unit at the Institute of Psychiatry, where much of Eiser's work in the late 70's was carried out. This in itself is sufficient to make the paper intriguing, but what is even more fascinating is the fact that virtually no mention is made of Eiser's mainstream attributional studies, that author receiving only passing mention as a subordinate author on two cited papers concerned with coping behaviours rather than attribution.

Finally, there is preplexing reference to three papers by Litman *et al* (1977 *op cit*, 1979 *op cit* and 1983) also from the Institute, which dealt with varieties of self-report including coping behaviours and the perceived effectiveness of such behaviours. In the Edwards *et al* paper, an attempt is made to recast these earlier studies as if they were primarily attribution papers, presumably on the grounds that they were concerned with people's stated reasons for such things as relapse and non-relapse. At the time of writing, however, the papers made little reference to attribution theory *per se*, and concerned themselves mainly with the analysis of clients' stated coping mechanisms. It seems likely that the principal authors thought they were dealing with events and behaviours, rather than with functional verbal reports. An example which illustrates this point can be found at the foot of page 534 in Edwards *et al*'s article. They write:

> '. . .the theoretical relevance of studies on coping behaviour which have been conducted by Litman and her colleagues (Litman *et al*, 1983) deserve note. These investigators administered a 'Coping Behaviours Inventory' to a sample of hospitalised alcoholic patients and then applied a Principal Components Analysis to a set of *attributions* relating to what in the past had seemingly helped these subjects to stay off drink.' (my italics – author).

The quote refers to the 'attributions' analysed in the paper by Litman *et al* (1983 *op cit*) but examination of the paper in question fails to uncover any mention of attribution or attribution theory anywhere within the text. Furthermore, it is clear that Litman and her colleagues were more concerned with their data as veridical statements than as attributions, at least insofar as attribution *theory* was concerned. For example, Litman *et al* concluded:

'. . . . . .the instrument could be used to indicate the degree to
which a patient's current coping style is varied and flexible,. . . .to
indicate the areas in which coping skills are already being utilised
so that these may be enhanced. . . . . . . .to isolate those areas in
which the patient is deficient in coping behaviours so that these
may be taught.'

It is obvious from the above that subjects' answers were being
regarded as indicants of actual world events and behaviours, rather
than as functional within the context of attribution theory. Consequently, the Edwards *et al* paper presents a slightly paradoxical aspect.

The study involved a sample of 66 'alcoholics', all male and married,
from an initial follow-up sample of 99, who completed an Attributions
Inventory. The style of the Inventory contrasts with the parsimonious
approach adopted by Eiser in his smoking studies (*op cit*), and consists
of no fewer than 70 items. Subjects rated each item on a five point scale,
indicating whether they felt the event or circumstance described in the
item had helped or hindered their ability to cope with their drinking.

The inventory itself is not readily identifiable as a measure of
attributional style in the way that, for example, the Seligman or Weiner
scales are. It is difficult to see links between certain of the items and
established attributional dimensions, the construction of the schedule
appearing to have more in common with the instrument used in the
earlier papers by Litman *et al*, rather than with later attributional
research. To some extent, therefore, the paper itself appears to be
attributional in interpretation rather than in conception; a fact which,
as we shall see, is not without significance.

Data analysis proceeds by way of regression; in this instance, the
70 items are formed into 11 clusters 'in terms of the original intention
of the questionnaire to tap different sectors of attribution.' Scores on
these 11 subscales are then factor-analysed, a procedure which produces two main factors labelled 'active' and 'responsive' respectively.
Finally, factor scoring takes place on these two factors, and the factor
scores are then correlated with a variety of outcome measures. A
number of significant and interesting associations emerge between the
'active' and 'responsive' factors and the outcome measures, suggesting
that within the data there are stable patterns of attribution which relate
to treatment success. On the basis of these results, the authors argue for
the inadequacy of the internal/external dimension in relation to the
issues with which the paper is concerned, and they suggest that their
own dimensions might give a better account of these, and by implica-

tion other, similar, data. It will remembered, however, that previous work from the same institution had already shown that a locus × stability interaction at least was necessary to make attributional sense of addiction, and that locus by itself was inadequate for this purpose.

In conclusion, the Edwards *et al* paper is notable since it finds further evidence of the link between styles of explanation and substance use. However, the implications go beyond this. The findings emerge from a lengthy questionnaire that is quite dissimilar in scope and content to the more standard attribution measures used by Eiser and others; yet consistencies are nonetheless found. Furthermore, the dimensions emerging from this large and sometimes unlikely (in attributional terms) item set still bear a marked resemblance to a locus × controllability interaction of the Weiner type, with 'active' implying personal control and 'responsive' implying reactivity to outside agencies. The Edward's *et al* dimensions are thus recognisable as mainstream attributional constructs, despite the fact that the items from which they emerge, generally speaking, are not.

Consequently, the study answers to some extent the criticism that attributions emerge from 'customised' attribution questionnaires simply because they were put there in the first place. Most importantly, it suggests that the functional nature of answers to questions is not restricted to the classical attributional formats, but can make a measurable impact on self-report data in a more general sense. Remember, the Edwards *et al* questionnaire draws heavily on a previous instrument that, at the time, was never intended to measure attributions *per se*.

Perhaps the most important insights arise, not from the paper itself, but from Edwards' reply (13th August 1989) to the author's letter raising the points discussed previously. With regard to the virtual omission of Eiser's smoking studies, Edwards concedes that a sharper focus might well have been given to those studies within the paper. However, Edwards' comments with respect to the Litman *et al* papers are more fundamental, and it is worth examining these in more detail.

Firstly, Edwards makes no attempt to disguise the fact that he tried to recast the earlier work in an attributional mould. Edwards states that, on re-examining Gloria Litman's work, he really came to think that it could be re-interpreted within an 'attributions' perspective, at least to an extent. Furthermore, Edwards explains, there is little evidence as to whether people who say that they employ particular coping styles or strategies to avoid relapse actually employ those techniques with any greater frequency or power than people who don't make such claims. Consequently, he concludes, we must be dealing with what people *say*, and to an extent with personal attributions, rather than with proven events on the ground. The puzzling aspect of the paper in appearing to look backwards methodologically to previous *non-attributional* research, whilst attempting to recast those studies in an attributional framework, is thus resolved. It apparently indicates a reappraisal occasioned by the fact that the results of a prior body of work had progressively come to have implications that were different from those envisaged at the time. With this in mind Edwards attempted to provide a functional re-examination of data which originally were almost certainly gathered for the veridical information they might yield. In so doing, he uncovered two attributional dimensions bearing a close resemblance to certain Weiner-type constructs which emerged from studies of a methodologically and substantively different type.

Finally, Edwards felt these two attributional styles might have different implications for the treatment success of more-dependent, as opposed to less-dependent, clients; though he was characteristically guarded in his conclusions:

> 'If our current findings are found to have broader applicability than to the particular sample with which we are working, the heuristic implication of establishing a connection between attribution and outcome domains may be important' (p.544)

Hammersley, Morrison, Davies and Forsyth (1990)

This final study resembles the Edwards *et al* paper in being primarily non-attributional in style and conception, but nonetheless illustrating an important link between behaviour and style of explanation at the end of the day. The study was fundamentally intended to illuminate the nature of the relationship between economically-motivated crime (theft) and drug use (primarily heroin and opioids).

Two related beliefs underly the assumption that heroin use *per se* is a sufficient cause of economically-motivated crime. The first belief is that heroin use rapidly and inevitably escalates to a level at which the cost of the drug massively outstrips the ability to fund it by legitimate means; the thousand-pound-a-week habit is often referred to in the popular media. The second belief is that heroin has properties which make it (along with cocaine) uniquely addictive, namely reinforcing effects which are so powerful that people cannot do without them, and withdrawal effects so horrendous that people will do anything to avoid them.

By these means, the drug 'forces' people into a life of crime and degradation. Within this context, the Hammersley *et al* study was carried out between 1985 and 1987 for the Criminological Division of the Scottish Home and Health Department, heroin use being of particular concern at that time. The study was published by the Scottish Office in 1990.

The data were derived from an interview, which typically lasted about one hour. It was a semi-structured but highly detailed schedule covering a variety of drug and crime-related variables, including information about income from all sources (both legal and illegal), expenditure on drugs and other things, details of extent and type of drug use, details of 21 classes of crime, and a number of finer-grained questions on these and other issues. Altogether data were obtained from 151 people, comprising 96 prisoners and young offenders in Scottish penal institutions, and 55 people not in custody, covering a range of types of drug use, and degrees of involvement with drugs. The aim was to obtain a prison sample at risk for drug use and crime, and a comparable non-prison sample, so the selection procedures for the non-prisoners reflected this aim and made extensive use of walk-in centres in Edinburgh and Glasgow.

On the basis of what had gone before, it was evident that there was little to be gained by investigating the issue solely and simply by asking drug users to provide reasons for their acts of theft. Such a method clearly might predispose to a particular type of functional explanation, whereby personal responsibility could be minimised by attributing causal agency to drugs. In addition to eliciting direct statements of causality, it was therefore also decided to collect information about drugs used, income required, income obtained, crimes committed and other related topics, with a view to using regression as a means of exploring possible causal relationships via statistical means. It will be recalled that whilst self-reports of consumption are of unknown validity in absolute terms (see chapter 8), their usefulness as discriminants in analysis has been demonstrated in a number of studies. Specifically, their usefulness in regression analysis as a means of testing possible causal links remains intact even if the absolute levels reported are prone to contextual artifacts.

We expected at the outset that subjects would wish to confirm a causal link between drug use and crime, since such a link would be functional for them. This in fact proved to be the case. *Subjects attributed their crimes directly to their drug use when the specific question was asked*. Given this fact, the subsequent failure to find a strong causal connection when alternative means of questioning and analysis were employed could not be explained in terms of motivational bias on the part of subjects.

During the interview, subjects were asked to recall a variety of behaviours, including extent of drug use and criminal involvement, keeping the reports separate as far as possible and using the retrospective diary technique for aiding recall. Regression analysis was then used to explore a number of hypothesised causal relationships between variables. In simple terms, regression analysis in this instance involved finding the extent to which such things as theft, violent robbery and other criminal acts could be predicted from other variables. In terms of popular belief, for example, one would expect that extent of theft amongst heroin users would be predicted most strongly by extent of heroin use. By examining the predictive power of different variables in this way, one can discover whether the actual pattern of prediction accords with expectation.

In the present instance, there was a particular interest in those variables that might predict crime, so data were obtained on a variety of possible predictors for inclusion in the regression equation. The variables used included information on six drug-use measures, eight measures of financial circumstances, three measures of social strain, six measures of friends' crime and drug involvement, plus age and social class, as well as information on five types of crime. The results from this analysis are shown in the pie-chart (Figure 2). It will immediately be observed that, of the variance explained (53.5%), the largest part (22.5%) is explained by use of opioids. Therefore, one can say that when viewing this sample *as a whole*, the best predictor of theft was involvement in opioid use. To the extent that this is true, the popular stereotype appears to be confirmed; theft was best predicted by involvement with opioids, mainly heroin.

However, the findings described above apply to the group *as a whole*. It now becomes important to examine the nature of a possible functional relationship between heroin (opioid) use and theft *within* the opioid-using group, excluding everyone else from the analysis. A simple causal relationship would then manifest itself in terms of ability to predict extent of theft from extent of heroin use within that group. That is, other things being equal (e.g. financial resources) heavier users ought to steal more than those who use less. The results of this analysis are illustrated in the pie-chart (Figure 3). It is at once apparent that the simple causal relationship between heroin use and crimes of theft which is implied by the popular stereotype does not accord with these results.

Firstly, we can see that the best predictor of crimes of theft amongst heroin users is not extent of drug use. Extent of use in fact explains only a small proportion of this variance (5.6%), whereas 20.5%, much the

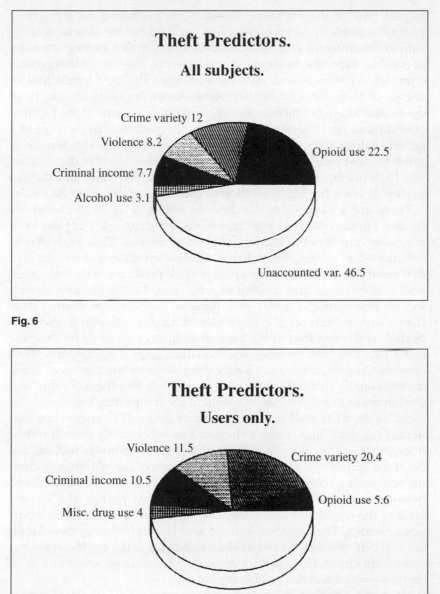

Theft Predictors.

All subjects.

Crime variety 12

Violence 8.2

Criminal income 7.7

Alcohol use 3.1

Opioid use 22.5

Unaccounted var. 46.5

Fig. 6

Theft Predictors.

Users only.

Violence 11.5

Criminal income 10.5

Misc. drug use 4

Crime variety 20.4

Opioid use 5.6

Unaccounted var. 47.9

Fig. 7

largest part of the explained variance, is explained by the 'crime variety' variable. In terms of the interview data, 'crime variety' was the sum of the different crimes committed and is thus a general measure of criminal expertise. In straightforward terms, this means that general criminal experience and involvement were the best predictors of crimes of theft *amongst* heroin users. Accordingly, the capacity of opioid use to predict theft in the whole sample was due to the fact that opioid users *per se* were more likely to have criminal experience of a general nature that were those who did not use opioids. This is not surprising since opioid use is most prevalent in areas of urban deprivation and high unemployment where crime is more common, and theft in particular is a more likely solution to economic problems of all kinds.

There are a number of conclusions which arise from the above results. Firstly, crimes of theft committed by drug users appear to be much like crimes of theft committed by anyone else. They are best conceptualised as crimes, rather than as disease symptoms. If it is the case that general criminal involvement is the best predictor of theft amongst heroin users rather than amount of drug used, theft in this group starts to look primarily like a way of solving an economic problem, rather than a drug-driven act of compulsion. Such a conclusion is also supported by the fact that in the present sample *crime predicted drug use better than drug use predicted crime*. Within such a framework, there appears to be no justification for treating thefts by drug users as being motivationally distinct from thefts committed by others. People will steal in order to get the money to obtain the things they want, and this includes drugs as well as other consumer items. (The suggestion that heroin-related crime is much the same as other crime should not be interpreted as an endorsement of any particular method of judicial disposal for crimes of theft. Stealing is a function of many things, including economic circumstances, educational opportunity, social situation, housing, available employment, and so forth, as well as of a learned view of the world and a functional set of attitudes that go with a particular setting. The point being made here is simply that crimes of theft amongst drug users do not appear to have a different motivational basis from crimes by non-drug-users. What one does about crimes of theft in general remains a separate issue.)

However, although the data from the above study reveal no simple relationship between heroin use and crime the argument cannot rest there. From a statistical point of view the idea of *sufficient cause* represents only on type of causal model, of possibly the most elementary kind. Furthermore, sole and sufficient causes are exceptionally rare where social behaviour is concerned. The idea that heroin *per se* is a sufficient cause of crime is thus probably naive from the outset, and parallels a similar simplistic theory of the relationship between alcohol and crime. In a sense, therefore, by concluding that heroin is not in itself a direct cause of crime we have merely disposed of a straw man.

The idea that alcohol causes crime in some direct way is a similar straw man, but one who is more readily identified as such for a very obvious reason. We can observe, without doing any research at all, that most people drink but most people are not criminals; alcohol cannot therefore be a sufficient cause of crime. However, with heroin the situation is reversed. Most people do not use heroin; and criminality is extremely common amongst those who do. Nonetheless, these differences in the distributions of the two activities should not blind us to the commonalities, namely that in both cases we are postulating direct links between use of a substance and a specific behavioural consequence in a manner which is syllogistic.

It has been suggested that the view of either alcohol or heroin as being sufficient causes of crime or theft is naive and does not stand up even to close *a priori* scrutiny. Nonetheless, the findings from the above study do not rule out a causal role for alcohol and heroin, in the context of a multi-factor causal model. In other words, given certain sets of social or economic circumstances and certain adaptive individual characteristics (beliefs, values or whatever), it remains entirely possible that alcohol and/or heroin may play an identifiably causal role in specified contexts, in terms of some mathematical model of causality. What this means is that we have to move to a more differentiated view of causality that involves seeing alcohol or heroin use as factors in a causal model comprising a number of factors. The data from the present study, for example, are compatible with the idea that a causal role for heroin might begin to emerge once the impact of differences in criminal experience and expertise are partialled out of the equation. They are also compatible with the idea that heroin use might in some indirect way *exacerbate* crime amongst those who are already involved in criminal activities. In the meantime, however, it remains clear that a view of heroin as a unitary and straightforward cause of crime is untenable. As a result, the simple attribution of crime to substance use by those in the present study has to be considered in terms of its possible value as a cognitive strategy for a group of people whose drug use has created legal and other problems for them.

In the present study, subjects' responses to direct questioning about their reasons for stealing did in fact evoke the stereotyped picture of the helpless addict forced to steal in order to support a habit which had taken over their capacity to resist; a drug-driven compulsion. Regression analysis, however, suggested that drugs were not the principal driving force behind the crimes. The answer to the direct question is thus revealed as primarily functional-within-context because it presents theft in terms of a *bad but non-volitional* interaction, which is more likely to elicit a favourable *attributional verdict* from salient others. It is indeed difficult to envisage why a rational person would answer in any other way in the circumstances.

McConnochie (1996)

Brief mention deserves to be made of two potentially important studies by McConnochie (1996) which are unpublished at the time of writing. McConnochie recruited a sample of problem drinkers through a local alcohol clinic, and a matched sample of non-problem (low consumption) drinkers. Both groups filled in a standardised dependency questionnaire. As would be expected, the problem drinkers produced significantly higher scores. Next, McConnochie asked the groups to reverse roles; that is, problem drinkers were asked to fill in the questionnaire after the style of a non-problem drinker, and non-problem drinkers were asked to answer the questions after the style of a problem drinker. ANOVA revealed differences between conditions, but no differences between groups. That is, either group could produce a set of responses not significantly different from that produced by the other (i.e. the non-problem-drinking group could produce a 'problem' script and the problem-drinking-group could produce a 'non-problem' script, as well as their own 'proper' scripts). McConnochie claimed to have shown that 'dependent' and 'non-dependent' scripts (patterns of responding) were available to both groups, in a manner that echoes the findings of the Anderson, Aitken and Davies study (*op cit*).

In the second, and more fundamental study, McConnochie recruited three groups of subjects. First she recruited a new group of problem drinkers attending a clinic for alcohol problems; second, a new group of non-problem (low consumption) drinkers; and third, a crucial group of heavy drinkers closely matched for consumption to those attending the clinic but NOT attending any clinic or agency. All three groups then completed a dependency measure. ANOVA showed a significant main effect for groups overall, but follow-up tests for planned comparisons showed no difference in dependency scores between the controls (low drinkers) and the heavy drinkers NOT in agency contact. By contrast, the group attending the clinic produced dependency scores that were significantly higher than either of the other groups.

McConnochie argued that, since dependent and non-dependent styles of verbal responding were shown to be equally available in the first study, the pattern of results in the second was consistent with the idea that agency contact was the factor that predisposed subjects to select the 'dependent' form of responding. By contrast, amount of alcohol consumed appeared to have little bearing on the results.

The Widening Perspective

In the last few years, a number of recent studies investigating the attributional nature of addiction have been carried out, whilst at the same time perspectives in drug use and attribution have been broadening. There have been a number of attempts to test predictions of attribution theory within the field of addiction, as opposed to attempts to test hypotheses about addiction making use of attributional theory, and not all of the former have been an unqualified success in terms of confirming well-known attributional hypotheses.

Thus Jenks (1994) found certain differences between the ways that smokers attributed their own smoking and the manner in which they explained the smoking of other smokers. Jenks' research was located very squarely within the classic paradigms of attribution theory, and not all the predictions of those theories were borne out. Specifically, the so-called 'fundamental attribution error,' whereby it was hypothesised that subjects 'would attribute their own smoking to external causes' (see Jenks, p.134) was not found. In fact subjects tended to offer addiction-type explanations for their own smoking, with little support being found for 'fundamental' attribution errors. However, the results from the study are by no means as surprising as Jenks perhaps implies. The sample derivation in the study is not particularly clear, consisting partly of students and partly of contacts recruited via students. For whatever reason the smokers in the Jenks study generally had negative views of their own habit. ('. . .respondents believed (a) that they are more likely than other smokers to perceive their smoking habit as dirty, (b) that other smokers think it is easier to quit than they do, and (c) that they are more likely than other smokers to believe that they are going to have major smoking-related health problems'). Such views are certainly not representative of the spread of views to be found in the population of smokers generally, and in Eiser's terminology they would be described as 'dissonant' smokers. In such circumstances, therefore, one could in fact predict from Eiser's earlier work on dissonant smokers that defensive or 'addicted' explanations would be found. Jenk's findings thus only appear problematic from an already discarded perspective, since where addiction is concerned, the 'fundamental attribution error' is not fundamental at all.

Certain aspects of attribution theory which were originally developed in artificial settings with hypothetical scenarios simply do not transpose without modification to the applied context. Thus Eiser (*op cit*; various) demonstrated over a decade previously that certain ingrained but unjustified assumptions about internal locus and responsibility (and reciprocally, about external locus and lack of responsibility) had little or no applicability where addiction was concerned *since helplessness could have an internal, as well as an external locus*. It is worth re-stating that researchers (e.g. Stuart, Borland and McMurray 1994) and students alike still regularly attempt to shed light on the addiction process via the attribution-like dimension of locus of control (Rotter *op cit*). It has already been noted that both internal locus and so-called dispositional factors which are normally seen as representing control or agency, can and frequently do work in reverse where addiction is concerned. *One can construct oneself in the role of prisoner of one's own internal constitution just as easily as prisoner of external forces or circumstances*; consequently the findings with respect to locus remain, and will always remain, ambiguous, unless locus is treated as an integral part of a pattern involving at least stability, and perhaps controllability also. It is thus unfortunate that some workers continue to use locus of control as a main outcome variable in studies of addiction, since Eiser demonstrated the ambiguity of this concept when used in the area of addiction over ten years ago.

On the other hand, there has been a welcome expansion in the perception of what may be legitimately subsumed under the heading of 'attribution'. Within this broadening perspective, attribution research can no longer be assumed to be a province defined solely by the classic paradigms. 'Applied attribution theory', if such a term may be deemed acceptable, is now much broader. Drug workers, clinicians, health theorists and others have now adopted and attempted to apply (with varying degrees of rigour and success) attributional principles in a variety of settings. A consequence is that there now exists a diverse and multifaceted body of evidence which, overall, shows or implies relationships between successful and unsuccessful resolutions to addiction problems, and measures or dimensions which may be seen as attributional in principle, or at least as having attributional implications.

For example, the highly regarded formulations of Prochaska and DiClemente may in some respects be considered to have an attributional aspect. They found, for instance, that heavy smokers and non-quitters were likely to have beliefs (cognitions) confirming the uncontrollability or addicted nature of their smoking behaviour, and their own lack of self efficacy with regard to quitting; and such beliefs are important components of Prochaska and DiClemente's 'Transtheoretical' change model. Thus in DiClemente, Prochaska, *et al* (1991) it was found that smokers preparing to quit had lower addiction scores on the Fagerstrom questionnaire (a measure of nicotine dependence; Fagerstrom 1978), higher reported levels of confidence to stop or maintain nonsmoking, and greater reported 'efficacy to abstain from smoking across various cues to smoke.' In an earlier study (Rossi, Prochaska and DiClemente 1988) it was also argued that heavy smokers might be encouraged to concentrate more on changing their cognitions about smoking until such time as they could contemplate quitting, before embarking on any processes of behavioural change ('Because. . .cognitive processes tend to be associated with decision making and the contemplation of change, the best recommendation for heavy smokers might be to concentrate on. . .cognitive processes until they are ready to change' p.7). Explanations based on feelings of uncontrollability and addiction are thus revealed as barriers to progress, rather than as simple statements of 'fact' without any motivational implication.

Whether it is fair to include Prochaska and DiClemente's work within the broadening remit of attributional research is very much a matter of personal taste. There are admittedly major differences between the theories in terms of their implications, especially with respect to notions of the status of verbal report and 'truth', and also with respect to the direction of apparent cause-and-effect relationships. Nonetheless, broadening the perspective on functional attribution can often reveal intriguing alternative possibilities; and also suggests that legitimate attributional interpretations of reported phenomena are not difficult to find if one is prepared to concede the possibility of their existence, and to look for them. From this wider viewpoint, it must be clear that an alternative explanation for many (most?) addiction phenomena is at least possible. Consequently, Prochaska and DiClemente's conclusion that particular patterns of cognitive (or to be exact, particular types of explanatory verbal reports) set the scene for particular outcomes in the sense that they are associated with greater or lesser degrees of success in quitting, can be located easily within the 'addiction as attribution' framework, even though the implications may differ. On a final note, it is worth referring to the influential work of Bandura (1986) and the useful notion of self-efficacy. The similarity between self-efficacy within Bandura's framework, and certain combinations of locus, stability and controllability in some attributional research (e.g. McAllister and Davies *op cit*) is so self-evident that the terms are effectively interchangeable in many contexts. It is now possible to refer to self-efficacy within the context of applied attributional research with scarcely a raised eyebrow in sight. Furthermore, there is in fact an empirical basis for this type of synthesis in an interesting paper by Grove (1993). This author examined the degree of correlation between self-efficacy scores and a number of variables that included the attributional variables of locus, stability, controllability, and globality. Small but significant correlations were found between self efficacy and controllability and stability. The author also makes use of a 'composite attributional index' combining behavioural self-blame and the abstinence violation effect!

The interested reader may find that other well-known and influential paradigms can be similarly accommodated under the umbrella of functional attribution, and that alternative interpretations of addiction phenomena are thereby suggested.

11

A Context for
Drug Problems

The preceding chapters have traced the development of attribution theory from early studies of the phenomenology of physical and social causality, through the contemporary formulations of Kelley, Weiner and others, to the notion of functional attribution and the idea that explanations can serve psychological purposes for the explainer. With respect to addiction, prominence has been accorded to the work of Eiser who showed how the type of explanation offered for using a drug varied predictably according to the nature of the drug use, as well as having implications for expectancies and future behaviour. It was also Eiser who suggested that, within a given society, the appropriate explanations for drug use were learned at the same time as the drug using habit itself was acquired.

To support these arguments, a number of studies have been cited illustrating the attributional nature of answers to questions. Whilst many of these studies were concerned with addiction, reflecting the subject matter of this book, it is a fact that most of the existing attributional evidence comes from groups of people with no drug or other problems. It is important to emphasise that making attributions is not a unique characteristic of drug users or other deviant groups, but a process that engages us all at various times. Consequently, it would be quite incorrect to visualise attribution as something in which problem groups engage, but which has nothing to do with explanations offered by non-problem, or 'normal', groups. The underlying processes are assumed to be common to all, within a given culture.

Attributions and Lies

It is also important to reiterate that attribution and attributional research reflect the manner in which explanations are derived and their subsequent functionality, but say nothing whatsoever about the validity or 'truth' of the explanations themselves. Attribution research clearly does not offer some way of discriminating between truth and lies; least of all does it represent a unique way of investigating the quality of the verbal reports of deviant or 'bad' people.

However, it seems that these essential facts about the nature of attribution theory are not always grasped, and the term 'attribution' is sometimes misused. For example, at a recent conference (October 1990) a speaker reported findings from a recent life-event study, in which people were interviewed about the possible causal role of stressful events in mediating psychological problems. A member of the audience questioned the validity of the data, which he was clearly entitled to do given the known problems in this area. But the precise form of the question was most revealing.

> 'Are these reports true, do you think?' he asked. 'Or are they just attributions?'

This type of confusion is fairly widespread. Due to a lack of appreciation of how attribution theory developed, and of the nature of the hypotheses that may and may not be derived from the body of theory, some individuals appear to employ the term simply as a user-friendly word for lying. The implication is that people either give true causal accounts of their behaviour OR they make attributions.

From such a standpoint, all manner of elementary confusions follow. For example, when asking regular drug users to explain their addiction (as in the Coggans and Davies study *op cit*) they must give addiction-type (internal-stable) explanations if they are to be truthful; otherwise they are just 'making attributions' (i.e.lying). And in the McAllister and Davies study (*op cit*), despite the clear functional shift revealed, the heavy smokers were 'telling the truth' at the second interview, whereas at the first interview they failed to do so (they just 'made attributions'). It appears that the failure to grasp the interactive nature of the cognition/behaviour dialectic leads to naive expectations that events will 'cause' verbal explanations in a direct way. For example, if drug users say they cannot stop using because they are addicted, that is simply because they *are*. If they say they crave their drugs, that is because they *do*.

Faced with this type of view, which sees behaviour and verbal reports as simple cause and effect, with deliberate falsification as the only mechanism capable of disrupting the connection, it is difficult to know how to make any further progress; yet the view is a popular one, and appears to underlie a good deal of questionnaire and interview-based research at the present time. The functional interpretive and constructive aspects of cognition and language appear to be denied, there are no shades of meaning, no awareness of nuance or of implication, no 'implicit theories', and equally-valid but alternative forms of representation simply do not exist. The assumption appears to be that people think in only the most rudimentary manner; there is only one reality, and people either represent it, or they tell lies. But perhaps most importantly, the entire symbolic-interactionist nature of language is ignored both historically and philosophically; language is downgraded to the level of a vicarious literal transaction whose only function is either to represent reality correctly, or else to deliberately obscure it.

By contrast, the functional attribution perspective indicates that human actions can be explained in a virtually limitless number of alternative ways; that the people to whom the explanations are addressed can be expected to make quasi-logical inferences on the basis of those explanations; and that by choosing one form of explanation rather than another, the explainer exercises a degree of control over the inferences that others will in fact make. The differing forms of explanation involved vary primarily in the emphases given to particular elements. For example, most human action comes about as a result of the interaction of a plethora of internal and external factors of various kinds; but by stressing particular subsets of these we can influence the conclusions arrived at by others. Within such a process, there is no sharp dividing line between truth and lies, so the application of such labels is arbitrary and subjective.

Where Does Truth Lie?

Attribution theory then explains certain things about the process of explanation, and permits the derivation of hypotheses which may be tested; but it reveals neither truth nor lies. With respect to explanations for illicit drug use, the present text argues that the passive and helpless state implied by the word 'addiction' derives from an 'implicit theory' (Ross 1989 *op cit*) which is primarily functional within a particular context, and that in other contexts people can and indeed do explain similar acts in terms which imply greater control and volition.

However, whilst addiction is revealed primarily as a functional form of explanation in a given context, from an attributional standpoint we cannot go further and assert that therefore people *really are* in control of their drug use simply because they report being in control in other contexts. Demonstrating that the state implied by the language of addiction is a functional form of attribution does not enable us to conclude that therefore a different form of explanation must be 'true'. If addiction and helplessness are functional in one context, then control and volition may be functional in another. Consequently, if we argue for the truth of either of the central styles of attribution, (i.e. on the one hand, a compulsion explanation, or on the other a volitional explanation of drug use) we make exactly the error outlined at the start of this chapter.

On the face of things, we have arrived at an impasse in which all that exists is functional explanation, with the real nature of the drug-using experience becoming if anything even more elusive than it was before. In fact, however, the answer to the riddle is obvious, if a little difficult to accept at first sight; namely, there is no single 'truth' to be found. The nature and consequences of drug use cannot be divorced from the contexts within which it takes place; the experience and social consequences of drug use are not fixed entities, but vary according to the social, legal and other sanctions that surround the activity. Consequently, the reports of drug users about their experiences and behaviour are primarily revealing about the circumstances and conditions under which drug use takes place, rather than revealing immutable and certain facts about the inevitable nature of drug use itself. In circumstances where drug users regularly behave like stereotypical junkies, and report that their drug use is beyond their capacity to control, we must therefore turn our attention outwards and try to identify those aspects of the social world that make such types of behaviour necessary, and that provide the functional basis for the accompanying reports of helplessness and addiction.

Drug Use and Context

The evidence from studies of the attributional nature of addiction implies that the meaning, experience and implications of using mind-altering substances vary according to context. In most of the experimental and quasi-experimental studies reviewed in previous chapters, the level of contextual variation achieved was usually only a trivial representation of the possible larger contexts for drug use; for example, a different style of interviewer, or a different label on a questionnaire. In the real world, these simple differentiations are represented by major structural components of the legal, medical and social systems within which drug use and misuse take place. Within a given context, the reality of drug taking assumes a particular form or 'social reality' (Cohen 1990). Change the context, and the reality also changes.

Consequently, a society has the capacity to create a drug problem in whatever image it wishes. Surrounding drug use by tougher legislation, longer and more frequent prison sentences (see for example Haw 1988), unhelpful health messages based on fear arousal (see Davies and Coggans 1991 *op cit*) and alarm and outrage in the media (see Royal College of Psychiatrists Report 1987 *op cit*) creates a system characterised by fear, moral censure, crime, and an escalating black economy. Within such a system, particular forms of explanation have survival value. Attribution studies of drug users show, in a microcosm, how such a context produces a form of 'addicted explanation' which is inextricably intertwined with that context. The story does not stop there, however. Attributional research shows how forms of explanation can be related to future behaviour and expectancies. Consequently, having created the circumstances within which a particular form of explanation is adaptive, we can reasonably expect consequences to flow from that form of explanation. Since a climate has been created, with respect to drug problems, within which explanations that remove personal responsibility are strategically the best, we would expect that services might be provided on those terms; and we could anticipate that users would then require to present themselves to agencies in the same terms in order to receive whatever benefit was to be had.

This seems to be exactly what has happened. At the present time, the services on offer are generally geared to providing for helpless drug addicts who use drugs 'against their will' and who are trying to stop. As a result, people who encounter problems stemming from their use of drugs tend to present at agencies in accordance with that agenda. However, many people familiar with illicit drug use at the street level rather than in the hospital or clinic setting, will be impressed by the fact that most users appear to take drugs on purpose because they enjoy it, and their immediate problems frequently arise from their desire to keep using rather than their desire to stop.

It is thus possible to argue that service provision is required of a type that caters for the needs of drug users wishing to continue, with a correspondingly lesser role played by 'stopping' services; a suggestion which is however in opposition to the prevailing ethos. By and large, the services required to help the majority of continuing users to function as well as possible remain scarce and under-developed, or else the province of isolated and charismatic characters whose motives sometimes appear uncertain. This is unfortunate, since there are reasons for supposing that services of this latter type are now required with increasing urgency.

Drug Use and AIDS/HIV

The link between intravenous (IV) drug use and HIV infection, with transmission of the virus from user to user occurring as a consequence of the use of contaminated needles which are shared, is well established (though the different dynamics associated with borrowing as opposed to lending still require more investigation). Furthermore, a government review body (Advisory Council on the Misuse of Drugs 1988) has concluded that HIV/AIDS represents a more serious threat to society than does drug use *per se*, a view with which many would concur. Consequently, policy on drugs has to reflect the need to control and contain the spread of HIV as a matter of priority, notwithstanding the other health risks associated with intravenous injection and the use of non-sterile equipment. The need for a 'new paradigm' in dealing with drug problems has been emphasised in detail by Stimson (1990) and there is no need here for a lengthy exposition of those arguments. It remains to say, however, that the IV drug use/HIV link has given new urgency to the need for services for continuing drug users, in order to monitor and as far as possible guide drug users in the direction of safe use. Such services clearly need to be user-friendly, non-censorious, and free from the risk of prosecution, or they will simply not be used.

This 'harm reduction' approach represents the best hope of limiting the spread of HIV into the general population via IV drug use, as well as controlling the other potential sources of harm that may arise. Services catering primarily for the needs of users who are trying to stop, and who are seen as helpless victims, clearly do not address the larger problem: namely, drug users wishing to continue with their use and consequently having no reason to contact existing agencies working to a *drug stopping* agenda. Something has to be done to draw this larger group into agency contact, where their drug-use can be monitored and their manner of use challenged if necessary, in the interests of personal and public health.

The basic agenda for such service provision requires users to take responsibility for the extent and manner of their use. But people can only be persuaded to use their drugs in a safer manner (e.g. smoke instead of inject) or a way that minimises the danger of infection (e.g. delay injecting until a clean needle is available) if in principle they are capable of implementing decisions about their drug use. If the prevailing view is one of helpless junkies driven by forces beyond their capacity to control, then any such attempt to alter drug use is rendered futile by the attributional style with which it is associated. Being 'addicted' is the antithesis of making and implementing decisions, and within such a framework people 'have to have' their drugs whatever the cost.

Addiction is therefore a specific subspecies of *learned helplessness*, a phenomenon which has been much researched in other contexts and has generally been found to hinder the individuals' attempts to take an active and constructive role in his/her own health-related behaviour. In particular, feelings of lack of control are associated with higher levels of experienced stress, and a general lowering in the ability to cope (see for example Fisher and Reason 1988; Fisher and Cooper 1990; Cooper and Payne 1988).

It is apparent that the increased responsibility expected from drug users in terms of making decisions about substances, sources of supply, routes of administration and lending/borrowing of needles, cannot take place within a framework which stresses a mechanistic view of the drug-taking process; that is, as an addictive process that happens to people, rather than something that people do. Such a view alienates people from their own behaviour and intentions. In order to cope with the decisions necessary to minimise the possible harmful consequences of drug use to self and to society, issues of volition and control, and thereby of *competence*, have to replace mechanistic conceptions. Progress can only be made along this route if the notion of addiction is seen for what it is; namely, a preferred style of explanation whose primary purpose is functional. It removes blame and responsibility in a climate of moral censure. However, that particular functionality is actually *dysfunctional* at another level. Whilst the addiction attribution minimises possible harm to the drug user deriving from the social and legal sanctions surrounding drug use, it does nothing to minimise the possible harm that might come from using drugs incompetently, and it reduces the likelihood of competent use. A new context for drug use is required within which a different set of attributions is functional, attributions that help the person to cope with the problems that may arise due to their drug use, rather than attributions whose function is to minimise the impact of the legal and social sanctions on drug use imposed by the society within which it takes place.

The involvement of HIV/AIDS with intravenous drug use now gives a particular impetus to the need for a drug-using context within which explanations in terms of volition and control are functional, types of explanation which have different implications for drug-using behaviour than currently-preferred explanations in terms of pharmacology and helplessness. People believing themselves to be helpless cannot guide or take responsibility for their actions; and the involvement of HIV with drug use now requires with some urgency that drug users do exactly that. In a society trying to limit the spread of HIV/AIDS via incompetent drug use, the addiction attribution is probably the single major obstacle to progress. It impairs the capacity to cope with the problems arising from unwise drug use *per se* and the ability to make and implement competent drug-taking decisions. The link between HIV and IV drug use now makes it imperative that if people decide to use drugs, and many people make that decision and will continue to do so, then they should use their drugs competently above all else.

Living with Drugs

Illicit drugs are probably not going to go away by themselves, and the possibility that a 'war on drugs' will succeed in eliminating them from our midst seems increasingly unlikely. History has shown us how prohibition can create more problems than it solves. At a time when borders are being dismantled and when international communication and travel are commonplace, the problems of trying to ensure that particular substances do not reach particular destinations are likely to increase rather than decrease. The problem is compounded by the fact that there are major economic incentives to overcoming whatever barriers are put in place; and the commodities themselves are easy to hide or disguise.

Consequently, the realistic option is the pragmatic one; learning to live with drugs whilst minimising the harm that some individuals may encounter with their use. Furthermore, in all probability drug use is going become more rather than less prevalent, a developing context within which harm reduction will make progressively more sense, whilst the drive to stamp out drugs will become increasingly out of touch and ostrich-like. In a world where experimentation with, and use of, illicit substances becomes more common, a framework is required which normalises this activity as far as possible, whilst providing users with the services they require in the interests of minimising harm, and controlling the spread of HIV and other infections. The alternative is a society in which an increasing number of people become sidelined in the 'helpless addict' role, unable to make decisions about their drugs or their manner of use, and unable to take part in that society on anything resembling normal terms; whilst the drive to eliminate the substances from our midst exacts an ever increasing toll in terms of societal disruption and the invasion of civil liberties.

It goes without saying that the approach being advocated requires some dynamic response; specifically it requires a step back from the worst excesses of the existing system, to a less punitive set of circumstances within which alternative forms of attribution may be encouraged to grow and eventually flourish. The two essential ingredients of any attempt to encourage drug use on terms which are controlled and manageable are, firstly, the belief that such control and management is possible; and secondly the belief that there are benefits to be had from adopting such an approach.

Addiction; A Systems Problem

Taken collectively, attribution theory and attributional research suggest that the current controls surrounding illicit drug use have had a determining influence on the way drug use is explained. In turn, the explanation has led to service provision of a type appropriate to the explanation itself, the explanation determining both the type of services offered and the terms on which drug users may present themselves. The last link in the chain occurs when drug users do in fact present themselves on those terms when they encounter problems, as the price of absolution. In other words, the functional attribution becomes the reality.

However, it is clear that in different circumstances, alternative forms of explanation could become functional; forms that would have different and more helpful implications for future behaviour. Given the extent to which drug use, and especially IV drug use, is now enmeshed with other critical health issues, the need for such a new reality could not be clearer. That alternative reality requires the development of a 'system' within which drug use is conceived of as an activity carried out for positive reasons, by people who make *individual* decisions about their substance use, and who may take drugs competently as well as incompetently. By contrast, the 'war on drugs' actually takes us in an opposite direction by repeatedly stressing that the only control possible over the use and misuse of illicit drugs is that imposed from outside.

It is clear that the problems created by the illicit use of mind-altering substances do not stand alone, but are part of a larger system. In the preceding paragraphs we have seen how the use and misuse of drugs is inextricably interwoven with other issues. Throughout this text it has also been repeatedly stressed that the explanations people offer for drug use are primarily functional in certain types of context, and consequently they change according to context. The problem of illicit drug use is thus basically a 'systems problem.' In describing addiction as a systems problem the word 'system' is used not in a general sense, but in the specific sense implied by systems theory (e.g. Ackoff and Emery 1972). Although a system may comprise most or all the elements of a set (in the sense that we all provide inputs to the addiction system), the focus is on the inter-relationships between the different identifiable components of the system, rather than on what goes on at any particular level. Systems theory also seeks to understand the manner in which changes at a specific point within the system can change the properties of the system as a whole, in the extreme case modifying the way the system works so as to change its outputs radically.

In the real world, it is possible to become so enmeshed at one particular level that one loses sight of the system within which one is operating, and when this happens one becomes blinkered to the larger context of which one is a part, perhaps even failing to realise that the changes made at that level can produce greater and perhaps non-beneficial effects on the system as a whole. To solve this type of problem requires analysis of the various parts, their susceptibility to manipulation, and prediction of the consequences of change for the rest of the system. Unfortunately, such a systems analysis is lacking for drug use and misuse. Nonetheless, it is apparent that in recent times the major focus has been on a particular component, a component that lays stress on the medical perspective, takes as its premise the presumption that taking illicit drugs is essentially an illness or an inadequacy from which harm must inevitably flow, and leads to the conclusion that treatment and prevention in various guises are the two most appropriate and most fundamental responses. In fairness, it must be acknowledged that this approach has not completely ignored the non-medical aspects, but nonetheless they are not accorded equal status, being merely suborned to the medical perspective as and when they appear to complement that part of the system.

The attributions people make for drug use, and the functionality that may be discerned from the study of how these change in different contexts, is the key to a realisation that the addiction system is not operating in a coherent manner. Coherence can be restored by taking the first steps towards a more systems-based approach, within which inputs from drug users and treatment specialists play a role as a necessary and essential part, but which accords equal status to historical and geographical factors, to political and governmental agendas, to the role of newspapers and television, the law, the broader social and political climate within which drug use takes place, up to and including everyone living within that social system, and the attitudes and values they learn, and which they bring to the issue.

Understanding the addiction system, as distinct from the medical problems of drug use, now requires a concerted effort to obtain a broader perspective from all parts of the system, followed by an effort to understand how actions at any one level, and which may appear advantageous at that level, can cause the overall output of the system to change in non-advantageous ways. In the preceding pages it has been argued that the functional use of the addiction attribution is a real and identifiable output, and as such it clearly demonstrates that the system surrounding the use and misuse of illicit mind-altering substances is not working in a helpful and productive way.

Without a change in perspective, we lay the foundations for a continuation of the drug problem *in the same terms*. We run the risk of making the problem more and more extreme, and consequently of coming to view counter measures of a progressively more arbitrary and socially destructive type as desirable and necessary, as we add more and more energy to the system, until eventually we transform a problem involving individuals taking mind altering drugs into a problem of life-and-death on the streets. Something like this appears to be happening both here and in the U.S.A. as the economic rewards of trading in the illicit drug-economy escalate in a never-ending spiral.

Addiction; Exploding the Myth

It is essential to be clear on certain points. It is not the message behind this book that the illicit use of drugs never creates problems for people. It is abundantly clear that numbers of people encounter serious health problems due to the unwise or careless use of mind-altering substances. This is true of drugs like heroin and cocaine; and it is also true of drugs like alcohol, tobacco and ben-zodiazepines (minor tranquilisers). To the extent that the use of illicit drugs is a danger to individual health, there is a problem. The extent of this problem is, however, generally overestimated at the population level, in comparison with the harm caused by the use of licit substances; and also in comparison with major health problems such as accidents at home and at work, child-pedestrian fatalities, heart disease and so on.

It is also clear that the incompetent use of drugs can cause damage within the family, the work group, within broader social networks, and that in some localities these problems assume a greater seriousness than in others. Whether it be the neglected spouse, struggling to cope with a growing family on resources depleted by a partner's gambling; the businessman embezzling in order to keep himself in claret; the factory worker whose drink or drug use materially affects his/her work performance; or the talented musician whose performance moves from the sublime to the grotesque in response to increasing heroin use; all these instances demonstrate that the thing we refer to as 'addiction' can have serious repercussions at both the societal and the individual level. Again, however, we have to note that whatever the activity or the substance, such problems are far from inevitable and that controlled use in particular contexts need have no implications whatsoever beyond that context. It is becoming increasingly clear that large numbers of people use drugs in a controlled fashion, never encountering serious problems with their use, and never coming to the attention of police, health or other authorities (Cohen 1990 *op cit*; Ditton 1990 *op cit*).

Finally, although it has been suggested that the understanding of drug action at the level of the cell is peripheral to the understanding of drug-related molar behaviours, the pharmacological effects are real: the particular pharmacology of a substance gives that 'addiction' is own peculiar quality, and humans and animals are aware of and can even recognise that quality under certain conditions. Furthermore, such differences account for the fact that certain substances are intrinsically more pleasurable to use than others, and hence are employed by people for their pleasurable effects whilst other substances are not. However, it is also the case that people can and do become 'addicted' to things that involve no external pharmacology, in the sense that they pursue an activity single-mindedly to the detriment of their personal health and the disruption of their family and social relationships; and it is also true that other people seem able to use substances that are pharmacologically potent on an extended take-it-or-leave-it basis with no long-term health consequences. Consequently, an external pharmacological agent is neither a necessary nor a sufficient condition to bring about that state we describe as 'addiction' amongst humans.

If substances themselves are not the crucial issue in the explanation of why people display 'addicted' behaviour, then there is clear need for a revision of basic strategy. We have to step back from the abyss towards which we are being beckoned not by users, but by those whose preferred solution to drug problems is to eliminate drugs and their use from our midst by whatever means appear necessary, no matter how socially disruptive this may be. Unless we seriously consider ways of reducing penalties, of producing more sensible media coverage, of reducing the political appeal of drugs, in other words of examining all aspects of the addiction system, the problem will metamorphose into something far more costly in societal terms. The response to the drug problem will come to have more serious, not to say lethal, consequences for society than the drugs themselves.

At the moment, the use of mind-altering substances serves as a springboard for responses to drug use that can eventually lead to death and chaos on the streets, where no such outcome is necessary. To avoid this outcome, it is necessary merely to take a more balanced perspective on the costs and benefits of illicit drug use; and in the light of that analysis, to arrive at the only sensible conclusion. Namely, it is time to abandon a response based on an escalating and ineffective tariff of legal sanctions against drug use; and switch to an approach which focuses on reducing the potential harm of certain incompetent drug-use practices, whilst handing personal control back to those who are involved. In other words, we need to rebuild our 'addiction system'; and in the process of doing so we may well discover that it was never in fact what we thought it was. We may discover that 'addiction' is not so much a thing that happens to people, as a functional set of cognitions surrounding the activity of taking drugs; a way of thinking made necessary only by the sanctions with which we surround the act of using substances to change our state of consciousness.

References

ACKOFF, R.L. & EMERY, F.E. *On Purposeful System: An Interdisciplinary Analysis of Individual and Social Behaviour as a System of Purposeful Events.* Trowbridge: Tavistock, 1972.

AITKEN, P.P. *Ten-to-fourteen-year-olds and alcohol.* Edinburgh: HMSO, 1978.

ADVISORY COUNCIL ON THE MISUSE OF DRUGS. *Aids and Drug Misuse, Part I.* London, HMSO, 1988.

ALEXANDER, B.K., BEYERSTEIN, B.L., HADAWAY, P.F. & COAMBS, R.B. Effect of early and late colony housing on oral ingestion of morphine in rats. *Pharmacology, Biochemistry and Behaviour,* 15, 571-576, 1981.

ALEXANDER, B.K., COOMBS, R.B. & HADAWAY, P.F. The effect of housing and gender on morphine self-administration in rats. *Psychopharmacology,* 58, 175-179, 1978.

ANDERSON, I., AITKEN, P.P. & DAVIES, J.B. Recall of the ordering of the symptoms of alcoholism, *British Journal of Clinical Psychology,* 20, 137-138, 1981.

ANDERSON, G. & BROWN, R.I.F. Some applications of reversal theory to the explanation of gambling and gambling addictions. *Journal of Gambling Behaviour,* 3(3), 179-190, 1987.

ANTAKI, C. A brief introduction to attribution and attributional theories. *In* Antaki, C. and Brewin, C. *Attributions and Psychological Change.* Academic Press, (1982), (Ch.1, 3-19).

ASCH, S.E. & WITKIN, H.A. Studies in space orientation: I. Perception of the upright with displaced visual field. *Journal of Experimental Psychology,* 38, 325-337, 1948.

ASCH, S.E. & WITKIN, H.A. Studies in space orientation: II. Perception of the upright with displaced visual fields and with body tilted. *Journal of Experimental Psychology,* 38, 255-477, 1948.

BALL, J.C. The reliability and validity of interview data obtained from 59 narcotic drug addicts. *American Journal of Sociology,* 72, 650-659, 1967.

BANDURA, A. *Social Foundations of Thought and Action: a Social Cognitive Theory.* New Jersey; Prentice Hall 1986.

BARNES, G.M. & WELTE, J.W. Patterns and predictors of alcohol use among 1-12th grade students in New York State. *Journal of Studies on Alcohol,* 47, 1, 53-62, 1986. (Cited in Casswell *et al.*)

BAR-TAL, D. The effects of teachers' behaviour on pupils' attributions: a review. *In* Antaki, C. and Brewin C., *Attributions and Psychological Change.* London: Academic Press, 1982.

BARTLETT, F.C. *Remembering: an experimental and social study.* London: Cambridge University Press, 1932.

BELSON, W.A., MILLERSON, G.L. & DIDCOTT, D.J. The development of a procedure for eliciting information from boys about the nature and extent of their stealing. *Survey Research Centre*: L.S.E., circa 1968 (undated).

BECKER, M.H., HAEFNER, D.P., KASL, S.V., KIRSCHT, J.P., MAIMAN, L.A. & ROSENSTOCK, I.M. Selected psycho-social models and correlates of individual health-related behaviour. *Medical Care*, 15 (suppl.), 27-46, 1983. (Cited in King.)

BEM, D.J. Self-perception theory. *In* Berkowitz (ed.): *Advances in Experimental Social Psychology*. Hillsdale: Erlbaum, 1972.

BEM, D.J. Attitudes as self-descriptors: another look at the attitude-behaviour link. *In* Greenwald, Brock and Ostram (eds.), *Psychological Foundations of Attitudes*. N.Y: Academic Press, 1968.

BLOOM, F.E. The Endorphins: A growing family of pharmacological pertinent peptides. *Annual Review of Pharmacology and Toxicology*, 23, 151-170, 1983.

BOWMAN, W.C. & RAND, M.J. *Textbook of Pharmacology*, 2nd ed. Cambridge: Blackwell, 1980.

BOZARTH, M. The pre-eminent role of animal studies in comparative substance use. *In*, Warburton, D.M., *Addiction Controversies*. London: Harwood, 1990.

BRADLEY, G.W. Self-serving biases in the attribution process: a re-examination of the fact or fiction question. *Journal of Personality and Social Psychology*, 36, 56-71, 1978.

BREWER, M.B. An information processing approach to attribution of responsibility. *Journal of Experimental Social Psychology*, 13, 58-69, 1977.

BREWIN, C. & ANTAKI, C. The role of attributions in psychological treatment. *In* Antaki, C. Brewin, C. (Eds.), *Attributions and Psychological Change*. London: Academic Press, 1982 (Ch.2).

BROWN, G.W. Meaning, measurement and stress of life events. *In* Dohrenwend, B.S. and Dohrenwend, B.P. (eds.) *Stressful Life Events; their Nature and Effects*. New York: Wiley, 1974.

BROWN, G.W. & HARRIS, T. Fall-off in the reporting of life events. *Social Psychiatry*, 17, 23-28, 1982.

BROWN, G.W. & HARRIS, T. *The Social Origins of Depression: a study of psychiatric disorder in women*. London: Tavistock, 1978.

BROWN, R.I.F. Reversal theory and subjective experience in the explanation of addiction and relapse. *In* Apter, M.J., Kerr, J.H. and Cowles, M.P. (eds.), *Progress in Reversal Theory*. Holland, Elsevier, 1988.

BROWNE, D. Crack. *The Observer*, Sunday, 24th July, p.15, 1988.

CASSWELL, S., STEWART, J., CONNOLLY, G. & SILVA, P. *A Longitudinal Study of New Zealand Children's Experience with Alcohol*. Alcohol Research Unit. School of Medicine, University of Auckland, New Zealand, 1990.

CHICK, J. & DUFFY, J. Application to the alcohol dependence syndrome of a method of determining the sequential development of symptoms. *Psychological Medicine*, 9, 313-319, 1979.

CHRISTIANO, C..J. *Psycho-social correlates of smoking behaviour and attitudes*. National Clearing House for Smoking and Health (unpublished) 1970.

CLARK, D. Discriminative properties of drugs of abuse. *In* Warburton, D.M. (ed.), *Addiction Controversies*. London: Harwood, 1990.

COGGANS, N. & DAVIES, J.B. Explanations for Heroin Use. *Journal of Drug Issues*, 18(3), 457-465, 1988.

COGGANS, N., SHEWAN, D., HENDERSON, M. & DAVIES, J.B. *The National Evaluation of Drug Education in Scotland*. Research Monograph 4. London: Institute for the Study of Drug Dependence, 1991.

COHEN, P. *Cocaine Use in Amsterdam in Non-Deviant Subcultures*. Amsterdam: University of Amsterdam, 1989.

COHEN, P. Desires for Cocaine. *In* Warburton, D.M. (ed.), *Addiction Controversies*. Harwood: London, 1990. (Ch.16)

COHEN, P. *Drugs as a Social Construct*. Amsterdam: UniversiTeit van Amsterdam, 1990.

COLTHEART, M., PATTERSON, K. & MARSHALL, J.C. (eds.) *Deep Dyslexia* (2nd edition). London: Routledge Keegan Paul, 1987.

CONWAY, M. & ROSS, M. Getting what you want by revising what you had. *Journal of Personality and Social Psychology*, 47, 4, 738-748, 1984.

COOK, C.C.H. The Minnesota Mode in the Management of Alcohol and Drug Dependency; Miracle, Method or Myth? Part II. *British Journal of Addiction*, 83, 735-748, 1988.

COOPER, C. & PAYNE, R. *Causes, Coping and Consequences of Stress at Work*. London, Wiley, 1988.

CRONBACH, L.J. *Essentials of Psychological Testing* (2nd Ed.). New York: Harper, 1960.

CURRAN, J. *K2 Triumph and Tragedy*. London: Grafton, 1989.

DAVIES, D.L. Stabilised addiction and normal drinking in recovered alcohol addicts. *In* Steinberg, H. (ed.), *The Scientific Basis of Drug Dependence*. London: Churchill, 1969.

DAVIES, D.L. Normal drinking in recovered alcohol addicts. *Quarterly Journal of Studies on Alcohol*, 23, 94-104, 1962.

DAVIES, D.L., SCOTT, D.F. & MALHERBE, M. Resumed normal drinking in recovered psychotic alcoholics. *International Journal of the Addictions*, 4, 187-194, 1969.

DAVIES, J.B. "Drugspeak": The Analysis of Drug Discourse. Reading: Harwood Academic Publishers, 1997.

DAVIES, J.B. Drinking in England and Wales: the latest news from OCPS. *British Journal of Addiction*, 84, 957-959, 1989.

DAVIES, J.B. Questions and answers in addiction research. *British Journal of Addiction*, 82, 1273-1276, 1987.

DAVIES, J.B. Alcoholism, social policy and intervention. *In* Eiser, J.R. (ed.), *Social Psychology and Behavioural Medicine*, Chichester: Wiley, 1982.

DAVIES, J.B. Life stress and the use of illicit drugs, alcohol and tobacco: empirical findings, methodological problems and attributions. *In* Warburton, D. (Ed.), *Addiction Controversies*. Harwood: London, 1990. (Ch.22)

DAVIES, J.B. & BAKER, R. The impact of self-presentation and interviewer bias effects on self-reported heroin use. *British Journal of Addiction*, 82, 907-912, 1987.

DAVIES, J.B. & COGGANS, N. *The Facts about Adolescent Drug Abuse*. London: Cassell, 1991.

DAVIES, J.B. & STACEY, B. *Teenagers and Alcohol*. London: HMSO, 1972.

DiCLEMENTE, C.C., PROCHASKA, J.O., FAIRHURST, S.K., VELICER, W.F., VELASQUEZ, M.M. & ROSSI, J.S. The process of smoking cessation; an analysis of precontemplation, contemplation, and preparation stages of change. *Journal of Consulting and Clinical Psychology*, 59, 2, 295-304, 1991.

DICKERSON, M.G. *Compulsive Gambles*. London: Longman, 1984.

DICKERSON, M., HINCHEY, J. & FABRE, J. Chasing, arousal and sensation seeking in off-course gamblers. *British Journal of Addiction*, 82, 673-680, 1987.

DIGHT, S. *Scottish Drinking Habits*. London: HMSO, 1976.

DITTON, J. *The Scottish Cocaine Research Group. Scottish Cocaine Users: Yuppie Snorters or Ghetto Smokers?* University of Glasgow: Update 6. Internal Memorandum, September 1990.

DORN, N. & SOUTH, N. Reconciling Policy and Practice. *In* Dorn and South (eds.), *A Land Fit For Heroin*, 146-169. London: MacMillan, 1986.

EDWARDS, G. & GROSS, M. Alcohol Dependence: provisional description of a clinical syndrome. *British Medical Journal*, 1, 1058-1061, 1976.

EDWARDS, G. The Alcohol Dependence Syndrome. *In* Edwards and Grant (eds.), *Alcoholism: New Knowledge and New Responses*. London: Croom-Helm, 1977.

EDWARDS, G., BROWN, D., DUCKITT, A., OPPENHEIMER, E., SHEEHAN, M. & TAYLOR, C. Outcome of alcoholism: the structure of patient attributions as to what causes change. *British Journal of Addiction*, 82, 533-545, 1987.

EISER, J.R. From attributions to behaviour. *In* Hewstone, M (ed.), *Attribution Theory: Social and Functional Extensions*. Oxford: Blackwell, 1983.

EISER, J.R. & GOSSOP, M. "Hooked" or "sick": addicts' perceptions of their addiction. *Addictive Behaviours*, 4, 185-191, 1979.

EISER, J.R., SUTTON, S.R. & WOBER, M. Smokers, non-smokers and the attribution of addiction. *British Journal of Social and Clinical Psychology*, 16, 329-336, 1977a.

EISER, J.R. & SUTTON, S.R. Smoking as a subjectively rational choice. *Addictive Behaviours*, 2, 129-134, 1977b.

EISER, J.R., SUTTON, S.R. & WOBER, M. "Consonant" and "Dissonant" smokers and the self-attribution of addiction. *Addictive Behaviours*, 3, 99-106, 1978a.

EISER, J.R., SUTTON, S.R. & WOBER, M. Smokers and non-smokers attributions about addiction; a case of actor-observer differences? *British Journal of Social and Clinical Psychology*, 17, 189-190, 1978b.

EISER, J.R. Discrepancy, dissonance and the "dissonant" smoker. *International Journal of the Addictions*, 13, 1295-1305, 1978c.

EISER, J.R. Addiction as attribution: cognitive processes in giving up smoking. *In* Eiser (ed.) *Social Psychology and Behavioural Medicine*. Chichester: Wiley, 1982.

EISER, J.R., van der PLIGT, J. & RAW, M. Trying to stop smoking: effects of perceived addiction, attributions for failure and expectancy of success. *Journal of Behavioural Medicine*, 8, 4, 321-341, 1985.

EISER, J.R. *Social Psychology*. Cambridge University Press, 1986.

FAGERSTROM, K. Measuring degree of physical dependence to tobacco smoking with reference to individualization of treatment. *Addictive Behaviours*, 3, 235-241.

FEATHER, N. & SIMON, J. Attribution of responsibility and valence of outcome in relation to initial confidence and success and failure of self and other. *Journal of Personality and Social Psychology*, 18, 173-188, 1971.

FINCHAM, F.D. & JASPARS, J.M.F. Attribution of responsibility: From man the scientist to man as lawyer. *In* Berkowitz, L. (ed.), *Advances in Experimental Social Psychology*, Vol.13. New York: Academic Press.

FINNIGAN, F. *Stereotyping in Addiction: an application of the Fishbein-Ajzen theory to heroin using behaviour*. Ph.D. thesis. University of Strathclyde Library, 1988.

FINNIGAN, F. How non-heroin users perceive heroin users and how heroin users perceive themselves. *Addiction Research*, 4, 1, 25-32, 1996.

FISHER, S. & COOPER, C. *On the Move: The Psychology of Change and Transition*. London: Wiley, 1990.

FISHER, S. and REASON, J. *Handbook of Life Stress, Cognition and Health*. London: Wiley, 1988.

FRIEDMAN, J. & HUMPHREY, J.A. Antecedents of collegiate drinking. *Journal of Youth and Adolescence*, 14, 1, 11-12, 1985. Cited in Casswell *et al*.

FRIEZE, I. & WEINER, B. Cue utilisation and attributional judgements for success and failure. *Journal of Personality*, 39, 596-605, 1971.

GALLISTEL, C.R., STELLAR, J.R. & BUBIS, E. Parametric analysis of brain stimulation in the rat. I. The transient process and the memory-containing process. *Journal of Comparative and Physiological Psychology*, 87, 848-859.

GILOVICH, T. Biased evaluation and persistence in gambling. *Journal of Personality & Social Psychology*, 44, 6, 1110-1126, 1983.

GODDARD, E. *Drinking and attitudes to licensing in Scotland*. London: HMSO, 1986.

GODDARD, E. & IKIN, C. *Drinking in England and Wales in 1987*. London: HMSO, 1988.

GONZALEZ, G.M. Time and place of first drinking experience and parental knowledge as predictors of alcoholism and misuse in college. *Journal of Alcohol and Drug Education*, 28(3), 24-33, 1983. Cited in Casswell *et al*.

GOSS, A & MOROSKO, I.E. Relations between the dimension of internal-external control and the MMPI with an alcoholic population. *Journal of Consulting & Clinical Psychology*, 34, 189-192, 1970.

GOSSOP, M. & EISER, J.R. The addicts perceptions of their own drug-taking: implications for the treatment of drug dependence. *Addictive Behaviours*, 7, 189-194, 1982.

GOSSOP, M. Compulsion, craving and conflict. *In* Warburton, D.M., *Addiction Controversies*, London: Harwood, 1990.

GOZALI, J. Control orientation as a personality dimension among alcoholics. *Quarterly Journal of Studies on Alcohol*, 32 (1A), 159-161, 1971.

GREEN, D.M. & SWETS, J.A. *Signal Detection Theory and Psychophysics*. London: Wiley, 1966.

GROVE, J.R. Attributional correlates of cessation self-efficacy among smokers. *Addictive Behaviours*, 18, 311-320, 1993.

HAMBURGER, H. *Games as models of social phenomena*. San Francisco: Freeman & Co., 1979.

HAMMERSLEY, R., MORRISON, V., DAVIES, J.B. & FORSYTH, A. *Heroin Use and Crime: a comparison of heroin users and non-users in and out of prison*. Scottish Office Central Research Unit Papers. 1990.

HASTORF, A.H. & CANTRIL, H. They saw a game: a case study. *Journal of Abnormal and Social Psychology*, 49, 129-134, 1954.

HAW, S. The sentencing of drug offenders in Scottish Courts. *Report to SHHD Criminality and Law Research Group*. SHHD Library, January 1989.

HEATHER, N. & ROBERTSON, I. *Controlled Drinking*. London: Methuen, 1981.

HEATHER, N. & ROBERTSON, I. *Problem Drinking: The New Approach*. Harmondsworth, Penguin, 1985.

HEIDER, F. *The Psychology of Interpersonal Relations*: New York: Wiley, 1958.

HEIDER, F. & SIMMEL, M. An experimental study of apparent behaviour. *American Journal of Psychology*, 57, 243-249, 1944.

HEWSTONE, M. Attribution theory and common-sense explanations: an introductory overview. *In* M. Hewstone, *Attribution Theory: social and functional extensions*. Blackwell: Oxford, 1983. (Ch.1, 1-24.)

HUME, D. *A Treatise of Human Nature*. 1739-40.

JAHODA, G. A cross-cultural perspective on experimental social psychology. *Personality and Social Psychology Bulletin*, 5, 142-148, 1979.

JAMES, W. What is an emotion? *Mind*, 9, 188-205, 1884.

JAMES, W. *The Principles of Psychology*. New York: Dover Publications, 1890.

JAMES, W.H., WOODRUFF, A.B. & WERNER, W. Effect of internal and external control upon changes in smoking behaviour. *Journal of Consulting Psychology*, 29, 184-186, 1965.

JELLINEK, E.M. *The Disease Concept of Alcoholism*. New Haven: Hillhouse, 1960.

JENKINS, C.D., HURST, M.W. & ROSE, R.M. Life changes: do people really remember? *Archives of General Psychiatry*, 36, 379-384, 1979.

JENKS, R.J. Attitudes and perceptions toward smoking: smokers' views of themselves and other smokers. *Journal of Social Psychology*, 134, 3, 355-361, 1994.

JESSOR, R., GRAVES, T.D., HANSON, R.C. & JESSOR, S.L. *Society, Personality and Deviant Behaviour*. New York: Holt, Rinehart & Winston, 1968.

JOHNSON, R.N. & JOHNSON, L.D. Intraspecific aggression in Siamese fighting fish, Betta Splendens. *Cited in* Johnson, R.N., *Aggression in Man and Animals*. Philadelphia: W.B. Saunders, 1972.

JOHNSON, T.J., FEIGENBAUM, R. & WEIBY, M. Some determinants and consequences of the teacher's perception of causation. *Journal of Educational Psychology*, 55, 237-246, 1964.

JOHNSTON, B.B. Treatment perspectives in drug misuse: the opiate paradigm. *In* D.J.K. Balfour (ed.), *Psychotropic Drugs of Abuse*. New York: Pergamon, 1990.

JONES, E.E. & DAVIS, K. From acts to dispositions. *In* L. Berkowitz (ed.), Advances in *Experimental Social Psychology*, 2. London and New York: Academic Press, 1965.

JONES, E.E. & NISBETT, R.E. The actor and observer: divergent perceptions of the causes of behaviour. *In* Jones, E.E., Kanouse, D.E., Kelley, H.H., Nisbett, R.E., Valins, S. and Weiner, B. (eds.), *Attribution: Perceiving the Causes of Behaviour*. Morristown: General Learning Press, 1971.

KELLEY, H.H. Attribution theory in social psychology. *In* D. Levine (ed.), *Nebraska Symposium on Motivation*, 15, 192-238. Lincoln: University of Nebraska Press, 1967.

KELLEY, H.H. & MICHELA, J.L. Attribution theory and research. *Annual Review of Psychology*, 31, 457-503, 1980.

KING, J. Attribution Theory and the Health Belief Model. *In* M. Hewstone, (ed.), *Attribution Theory: Social and Functional Extensions*. Oxford: Blackwell, 1983.

KINKADE, K. *A Waldon Two Experiment*. New York: Morrow, 1973.

KNIGHT, I. & WILSON, P. *Scottish Licensing Laws*. London: HMSO, 1980.

KUHN, T.S. *The Structure of Scientific Revolutions, 2nd ed.* Chicago: University of Chicago Press, 1970.

LADER, M. *Introduction to Psychopharmacology*. Michigan: Upjohn, 1983.

LANGER, E.J. The illusion of control. *Journal of Personality and Social Psychology*, 32, 2, 311-328, 1975.

LATANE, B. & DARLEY, J.M. *The Unresponsive Bystander: Why Doesn't He Help?* New York: Appleton Century Crofts, 1970.

LICHTENSTEIN, E. & KEUTZER, C.S. Further normative correlation data on the internal-external (I-E) control of reinforcement scale. *Psychological Reports*, 21, 1911-1916, 1967.

LILIENFELD, A.M. Emotional and other selected characteristics of smokers. *Journal of the National Cancer Institute*, 22, 259-282, 1959.

LITMAN, G., EISER, J.R., RAWSON, S.B. & OPPENHEIM, A.N. Towards a typology of relapse: a preliminary report. *Drug and Alcohol Dependence*, 2, 157-162, 1977.

LITMAN, G., EISER, J.R., RAWSON, S.B. & OPPENHEIM, A.N. Differences in relapse precipitants and coping behaviour between alcohol relapsers and survivors. *Behaviour Research and Therapy*, 17, 89-94, 1979.

LITMAN, G.K., STAPLETON, J., OPPENHEIM, A.N. & PELEG, M. An instrument for measuring coping behaviours in hospitalised alcoholics; implications for relapse prevention treatment. *British Journal of Addiction*, 78, 269-276, 1983.

LOCHEL, E. Sex differences in achievement motivation. *In* Jaspars, J., Fincham, F.D., Hewstone, M. (eds.), *Attribution Theory and Research: Conceptual, Developmental and Social Dimensions*. London: Academic Press, 1983.

MCALLISTER, P. & DAVIES, J.B. Attributional bias as a function of clinical classification. *Drug Issues*, 22, 1, 139-153, 1992.

MCKENNELL, A.C. Bias in the reported incidence of smoking in children. *International Journal of Epidemiology*, 9, 167-177, 1980.

MACARTHUR, R.S. An experimental investigation of persistence in secondary school boys. *Canadian Journal of Psychology*, 8, 42-55, 1955.

MACHAN, T.R. *The Pseudo-science of B.F. Skinner*. New York: Arlington House, 1974.

MACRAE, J.R. & SIEGEL, S. Differential effects of morphine in self-administering and yoked-control rat. *In* D.J.K. Balfour, *Psychotropic Drugs of Abuse*. New York: Pergammon, 1990, p.81.

MALKIN, D. An empirical investigation into some aspects of problem gambling. Masters Thesis; University of Western Australia 1981. *Cited in* Dickerson, M.G.; *Compulsive Gamblers*. London: Longman 1984.

MARLATT, A. & GORDON, J.R. *Relapse Prevention*. New York: Guilford, 1955.

McCONNOCHIE, F. *Attitudes and Perceptions towards Alcohol and Addiction: a Socio-Cognitive Approach*. Ph.D. thesis (in progress). Department of Psychology, University of Strathclyde, Glasgow, 1996.

MICHOTTE, A. La Perception de la Causalite. *In* Vernon, M.D. *Experiments in Visual Perception*. London: Penguin, 1946. (p.261)

MILES, T.R. & MILES, E. *Help for Dyslexic Children*. London: Methuen, 1983.

MILLER, D.T. & ROSS, M. Self-serving biases in the attribution of causality. Fact or fiction? *Psychological Bulletin*, 82, 213-225, 1975.

MUGFORD, S.K. & O'MALLEY, P. Policies Unfit for Heroin? A Critique of Dorn and South. *International Journal on Drug Policy*, 2, 1, 16-22, 1990.

NADRITH, M.P. Locus of control and drinking pattern in army trainees. *Journal of Consulting and Clinical Psychology*, 43, 96, 1975.

NEWCOMBE, R.D. & RUTTER, D.R. Ten reasons why ANOVA theory and research fail to explain attribution processes. 1. Conceptual Problems. *Current Psychological Reviews*, 2, 95-108, 1982a.

NEWCOMBE, R.D. & RUTTER, D.R. Ten reasons why ANOVA theory and research fail to explain attribution processes. 2. Methodological Problem. *Current Psychological Reviews*, 2, 153-170, 1982b.

NICHOLS, J.R., HEADLEE, C.P. & COPPOCK, H.W. Drug Addiction I. Addiction by escape training. *Journal of the American Pharmacological Association*, 45, 788-791, 1956.

O'DOHERTY, F. *The effect of naturally occurring life events on changes in consumption of alcohol, tobacco and heroin*. Ph.D. thesis. University of Strathclyde Library, 1988.

O'DOHERTY, F. & DAVIES, J.B. Life events and addiction: a critical review. *British Journal of Addiction*, 82, 127-137, 1987.

O'DOTHERTY, F. & DAVIES, J.B. Life events, stress and addiction. *In* Fisher, S. and Reason, J. (eds.), *Handbook of Life Stress, Cognition and Health*. Chichester: Wiley, 1988.

OGDEN, J. & WARDLE, J. Control of eating and attributional style. *British Journal of Clinical Psychology*, 29, 445-446, 1990.

OLDMAN, D. Compulsive gamblers. *Sociological Review*, 26, 349-71, 1978.

ORFORD, J. *Excessive Appetites*. London: Wiley, 1984.

PEMBERTON, C. The closure factors related to temperament. *Journal of Personality*, 21, 159-175, 1952.

PETERSON, C., SEMMEL, A., VONBAEYER, C., ABRUMSUN, L.Y., METALSKY, G.I. & SELIGMAN, M.E.P. The Attribution Style Questionnaire. *Cognitive Research and Therapy*, 6, 287-300, 1982.

PILIAVIN, I.M., RODIN, J. & PILIAVIN, J.A. Good Samaritanism: an underground phenomenon? *Journal of Personality and Social Psychology*, 13, 289-299, 1969.

PLANT, M.A., PECK, D. & SAMUEL, E. *Alcohol, drugs and school leavers*. London: Tavistock, 1985.

POPPER, K. *The Logic of Scientific Discovery*. Hutchinson: London, 1959.

POULTON, E.C. *Bias in Quantifying Judgements*. Sussex: Erlbaum, 1989.

POULTON, E.C. The new psychophysics: Six models for magnitude estimation. *Psychological Bulletin*, 69, 1-19, 1968.

QUIN, V. & MACAUSLAN, A. *Dyslexia: What Parents Ought to Know*. London: Penguin, 1986.

ROSECRANCE, J. Adapting to failure: the case of horse race gamblers. *Journal of Gambling Behaviour*, 2, (2), 81-94, 1986.

ROSENSTOCK, I. Why people use health services. *Millbank Memorial Fund Quarterly*, 44, 94-127, 1966. (Cited in King 1983)

ROSENSTOCK, I. The Health Belief Modal and Preventive Health Behaviour. *Health Education Monographs*, 2, 354-386.

ROSSI, J.S., PROCHASKA, J.O., & DiCLEMENTE, C.C. Processes of change in heavy and light smokers. *Journal of Substance Abuse*, 1, 1-9, 1988.

ROSS, L. The Interactive Psychologist and his Shortcomings: Distortions in the Attribution Process. *In* L. Berkowitz (ed.) *Advances in Experimental Social Psychology*, Vol.10. New York: Pergamon, 1977.

ROSS, M. Relation of implicit theories to the construction of personal histories. *Psychological Review*, 96, 2, 341-357, 1989.

ROTTER, J.B. Generalised expectancies for internal versus external control of reinforcement. *Psychological Monographs*, 80, 1, 1966.

ROYAL COLLEGE OF PSYCHIATRISTS *Alcohol: Our Favourite Drug*. London: Tavistock, 1986.

ROYAL COLLEGE OF PSYCHIATRISTS *Drug Scenes*. London: Graskell, 1987.

SCHMID, I., SCHARFETTER, C. & BINDER, J. Lebensereignisse in Abhangigkeit von Soziodemographischen Variablen. *Social Psychiatry*, 16, 63-68, 1981.

SHAVER, K.G. *The Attribution of Blame*. New York: Springer-Verlag, 1985.

SKINNER, B.F. *Beyond Freedom and Dignity*. Harmondsworth: Pelican, 1973.

SKINNER, B.F *About Behaviourism*. London: Jonathan Cape, 1974.

SKINNER, B.F. *Reflection on Behaviourism and Society*. New Jersey: Prentice Hall, 1978.

SKINNER, B.F. *Walden Two*. New York: Macmillan, 1948, 1976.

STEWART, J., DE WIT, H., & EIKELBOOM, R. Role of unconditioned and conditioned drug effects in the self-administration of opiates and stimulants. *Psychological Review*, 91, 251-268, 1984.

STEWART, R.M. & BROWN, R.I.F. An outcome study of gamblers anonymous. *British Journal of Psychiatry*, 152, 284-288, 1988.

STIMSON, G.V. AIDS and HIV: the challenge for British drug services. *British Journal of Addiction*, 85, 329-339, 1990.

STIMSON, G. & OPPENHEIMER, E. *Heroin Addiction*. London: Tavistock, 1982.

STOTT, D.H. Some psychosomatic aspects of casualty in reproduction. *Journal of Psychosomatic Research*, 3, 42-45, 1958.

STRAITS, B.C. & SECHREST, L. Further support of some findings about characteristics of smokers and non-smokers. *Journal of Consulting and Clinical Psychology*, 27, 282, 1973.

STUART, K., BORLAND, R. & McMURRAY, N. Self-efficacy, health locus of control, and smoking cessation. *Addictive Behaviours*, 19, 1, 1-12, 1994.

THOMPSON & OSTLUND, W. Susceptibility to readdiction as a function of the addiction and withdrawal environments. *Journal of Comparative & Physiological Psychology*, 60, 388-392, 1965.

TOTMAN, R. Philosophical foundations of attribution therapies. *In* Antaki, C. and Brewin, C. (eds.), *Attribution and Psychological Change*. London: Academic Press, 1982. (Ch.3)

VAN DER PLIGT, J. & EISER, J.R. Actors and observers attributions, self-serving bias and positivity bias. *European Journal of Social Psychology*, 13, 95-104, 1983.

VERNON, M.D. *Experiments in Visual Perception*. Penguin: Harmondsworth, 1966.

WANN, T.W. (ed.) *Behaviourism and Phenomenology. Contrasting bases for modern psychology*. London: University of Chicago Press, 1964.

WATSON, P. *War on the Mind*. London: Hutchinson, 1978.

WEARY, G. Examination of affect and egotism as mediators of bias in causal attributions. *Journal of Personality and Social Psychology*, 38, 348-357, 1980.

WEINER, B. *Achievement Motivation and Attribution Theory*. N. Jersey: General Learning Press, 1974.

WEINER, B., FRIEZE, I., KUKLA, A., REED, L., REST, S. & ROSEN BAUM, R.M. Perceiving the causes of success and failure. *In* E.E. Jones *et al* (eds.), *Attribution: Perceiving the Causes of Behaviour*. New Jersey, GLP, 1971.

WEST, R.W. & KRANZLER, H.R. Craving for cigarettes and psychoactive drugs. *In* Warburton, D. (ed.), *Addiction Controversies*. London: Harwood, 1990.

WHEELER, H. (ed.) *Beyond the Punitive Society*. London: Wildwood House, 1973.

WHITE, F. Cocaine and Mesoaccumbens dopamine neurotransmission. *In* D.M. Warburton, *Addiction Controversies*. Harwood: London, 1990.

WHITTAKER, E.M. Dyslexia and the flat earth. *Bulletin of the British Psychological Society*, 35, 97-98, 1982.

WILSON, P. *Drinking in England and Wales*. London: HMSO, 1980.

WISE, R.A. The role of reward pathways in the development of drug dependence. *In* Balfour, D.J.K., *Psychotropic Drugs of Abuse*. New York: Pergamon, 1990.

WITKIN, H.K. & ASCH, S.E. Studies in space orientation: III Perception of the upright in the absence of a visual field. *Journal of Experimental Psychology*, 38, 603-614, 1948.

WITKIN, H.A. & ASCH, S.E. Studies in space orientation: IV. Further experiments on perception of the upright with displaced visual fields. *Journal of Experimental Psychology*, Vol.38, 762-782, 1948.

WITKIN, H.A. & GOODENOUGH, D.R. Cognitive Styles: Essence and Origins. *Psychological Issues*. Monograph 51. New York: International Universities Press Inc., 1981.

WONG, G. The obsessional aspects of compulsive gambling. Society for the Study of Gambling. London 1980. *In* Dickerson, *Compulsive Gamblers*. London: Longman, 1984.

Index